SPIRITUAL WARF

Combo

By Alisha Anderson

Copyright ©2011 by Alisha Anderson

ISBN-13: 978-1501084102
ISBN-10: 1501084100

Alisha Anderson

P.O. Box 15716

Durham, NC 27704

Scripture quotations marked NET are from the Holy Bible,
New English Translation
Scripture quotations marked KJV are from King James
Version
Copyright © 1987 printing All rights reserved.

Scripture quotations marked NET are from the Holy Bible,
New English Translation

Prayer points:

Dr. Daniel K. Olukoya

Dr. Alisha Anderson

Table of Contents

DEDICATION

I love the LORD, for he heard my voice; he heard my cry for mercy. Because he turned his ear to me, I will call on him as long as I live. Ps 116:1-2 (NIV)
I praise God for my son, who has encouraged me in more ways than he will ever know.

This book is dedicated to Dr. Daniel K. Olukoya, General Overseer of Mountain of Fire and Miracle Ministries, Lagos, Nigeria. You gave me an opportunity to change my destiny because you heeded the Voice of God. The lessons I have learned from your teachings changed my life forever. I will be forever grateful.

I would like to thank God for the assignment to write this book. Many times we do not fully understand our assignments in its entirety. It's during these times that we must say "Lord let your will be done in my life". Knowing that all things work together for the good of those who love him, who have been called according to his purpose. Romans 8:28.

Chapter 1

In the U.S. Military, there are rules that service men must follow called the Geneva Convention. The Geneva Convention and their additional protocols are at the core of international law since they set the regulations on the conduct of warfare. They are designed to protect citizens who are not taking part in the war directly. In other words, they specifically protect people such as health and Red Cross personnel; occupants of schools and so on.

However, on September 11, 2001, for 102 minutes, the country was at war and the terrorist invaded a non-combative area. We can all remember how the world looked on in horror as terrorists flew hijacked passenger planes into New York City's mighty Twin Towers destroying this iconic building and killing more than 2, 700 people. The Geneva Convention was not adhered to, and no one was prepared for this holocaust.

In addition, in the spiritual realm and by extension our dreams the rules of the Geneva Convention do not matter.

In the war that I am speaking about all the action takes place in the heavenlies. There are no rules to protect people who choose not to participate in the war. More importantly, everyone is a part of the war, whether active or passive just as in a dream, and this is why we should always be prepared. Yes, unlike the innocent bystanders in the physical world God has armed us with weapons for combat.

Those who are passive and choose not to fight back will suffer defeat unless someone is covering them in prayer. The passive and blasé do not understand the importance of spiritual warfare and dreams. The bible tells us "my people are destroyed for lack of knowledge." Individuals who choose not to be bothered even because of ignorance can be "destroyed for lack of knowledge". You may argue that people cannot be ignorant to the devil's demise if they sit back passively and let their lives pan out, but I am here to tell you, without a doubt, that they do. These individuals lack knowledge because they do not recognize the consequence of refraining themselves from countering satanic attacks.

Most people have family and friends who may be considered as being collective captives. They are the ones who will tell you "it does not take all of that praying" or question if "you actually believe that stuff" or scornfully echo, "Everything with you is Jesus, Jesus, Jesus". These are the same individuals who believe that God will take care of them although they do not do anything but sit and wait on the Lord. These are the collective captives who believe solely in fate and lament that they cannot change anything. Sadly, these are the same people who do not believe God exists and can move mountains.

In other words, collective captives are "oblivious" that they are prisoners. They live in denial and choose to do nothing because they are content with "life" as they call it. They are unable to comprehend because they are carnal. Sometimes, they are also afraid of venturing into the "unknown". However, if you have family members or friends who have been taken captive by the enemy, there is hope.

Isaiah 49:24-26 asks the question "[c]an spoils be taken from a warrior, or captives be rescued from a conqueror?" "Indeed," says the Lord, "captives will be taken from a warrior; spoils will be rescued from a conqueror. I will oppose your adversary and I will rescue your children." (NIV)

This is good news for us because our God will fight for us; we have liberty and victory in Christ Jesus! "The spirit of the sovereign Lord is upon me because the Lord has chosen me. He has commissioned me to encourage the poor, to help the brokenhearted to decree the release of captives, and the freeing of prisoners." (Is 61:1.)

We must remember that this war is spiritual. It cannot be seen in the natural until it comes into manifestation. The battle is won or lost before you see it manifested in the physical. Many Christians suffer defeat wondering why life has turned out a certain way for them, and this is why I have written this book! The purpose of this book is to raise your awareness about attacks directed against you in your dreams.

Dreaming is an area we do not seemingly have authority over. This is why many people are eager to have the interpretation of their dreams. They want to be able to 'foresee' what will happen in 'their future' or perhaps understand the meaning of the dream. If the dreams are positive, they are happy, but when their dreams are negative they become fearful and either hopes for the best or find some unorthodox way to prevent misfortune from happening. We cannot continue to do absolutely nothing concerning our dreams. Yes, I said nothing. Having the interpretation of your dream solely is nothing. You also need Wisdom on what to do. A large percentage of people fail to cancel their dreams properly, and make statements such as "the devil is a liar". Well, we know the devil is a liar why waste time on the obvious. The first crucial step is to cancel the dreams specifically. We must understand that unchallenged negative dreams will only produce a negative harvest. We must not just say general prayers or praying amiss, wasting bullets (Prayer) by hitting the wrong targets.

We need to put on our spiritual armor and send air strikes against the powers afflicting us in our sleep. It is imperative that we cancel demonic dream attacks and break any covenants that might have been formed. Did you know that you could be initiated into witchcraft in your sleep? How? If you attend witchcraft meetings, cook in a witchcraft pot, walk in a river or deep ocean water to attend a meeting that's how. You may also be serving witchcraft foods too. Now, many of you may say you do not have those types of dreams. Well, you could be having those types of dreams and do not recall! I do not want you to get offended, but the notion that what you don't know can't hurt you will never work here. The more you pray serious warfare prayers or prayer points challenging evil powers, ask God to reveal to you what you are fighting against. Once God speaks to you and reveals the power behind your problem, you can now hit the specific target with perfection. Bulls-Eyes!!!

What's in a Dream?

I once had a dream in which I entered a restaurant and casually placed an order. I noticed that once my food had been prepared, a lady was putting a black powdered substance on my food. I could tell by her movement that she was being deceitful. So I boldly asked why she was putting the black substance on my food and couldn't help but notice that dead cockroaches had also been camouflaged into the food. I rejected the food, made it clear they could keep it and woke up.

This dream may appear quite harmless since I didn't partake in the "food", but these are the strategies of dream invaders (demonic agents practicing witchcraft manipulation while people sleep). There was something alarming about the dream, and it should have been seen as a warning of the sort since there were people in it who seemingly wanted to hurt me. Dreams about eating plant sickness, Luke warmness, miscarriages and initiations into witchcraft, which should not be taken likely. We should be on the offensive vs. the defensive.

There are many people who are conducting rituals, going to witchcraft meeting, and bowing down to evil altars in their sleep. They perhaps write off these dreams as being strange and move on with their lives. This is what the enemy wants and he uses that unprotected door to find different ways to possible pollute the lives of God's people.

Furthermore, don't be fooled like many Christians who believe that because they have given their lives to Jesus, they cannot have an evil spirit. Its deception and denial that keeps people in bondage and defeated. Deliverance dispels demons and break evil covenants and soul ties. Once a person experience deliverance from an evil spirit, it's refreshing and peaceful. Deliverance helps you to close demonic doors in your life. Deliverance is key to dealing with these types of spiritual issues. We should be receptive to deliverance and not try to avoid it at all cost. We must search ourselves and through sanctification purge out every evil plantation.

This is why it is so very important that we terminate and defuse every evil agenda of the enemy to divert our destinies.

For though we live in the world, we do not wage war as the world does. The weapons we fight with are not the weapons of the world. On the contrary, they have divine power to demolish strongholds. We demolish arguments and every pretension that sets itself up against the knowledge of God, and we take captive every thought to make it obedient to Christ." (2 Corinthians 10:3-5)
As such, we must be dressed for the battle and ready for war:

Finally, be strong in the Lord and in his mighty power. Put on the full armor of God so that you can take your stand against the devil's schemes. For our struggle is not against flesh and blood, but against the rulers, against the authorities, against the powers of this dark world and against the spiritual forces of evil in heavenly realms. (Eph. 6:10-12.)

"Have you ever given orders to the morning, or shown the dawn its place. Job 38:12 Most Christian intercessors and prayer warriors understand that during the hours of 12 a.m. - 4a.m. the Kingdom of Darkness conducts abominable acts that are forbidden by God. During this time they are speaking curses, incantations, planting afflictions into the lives of Christians by evil projections and manipulations of dreams. These are the devices of those speaking incantations and pronouncing curses.

The enemy should be afraid to confront us or at least know we know "to whom we belong and that we have the authority of God the Almighty." It is essential that we guide our mornings by commanding the elements (Sun, Moon, and Stars) to carry its affliction back to the senders. We must make sure we are taking our authority in Jesus Christ~ our Lord, Savior and Protector.

Prayer points:
I command the sun, moon, and stars to reject every enchantment against me and my family, in Jesus' name. Amen.

I command the sun, moon, and stars to vomit every enchantment against me, my husband, my children, etc. in Jesus' name. Amen.

Additionally, we should not forget the fact that dream warfare can also come from within your own household. I have written a book called "Dismantling Household Witchcraft" which explains how to deal with family members and those who are close to you who operated in witchcraft. If we have family members who participate in occult practices such as tarot cards, horoscopes, Ouija boards or demonic games their spirit can fight against you during the night while you are sleeping. They (those family members who participate in such) have covenanted with the demonic realm. Previously, I mentioned covenants and initiations through dreams and I would like to reiterate. If a person has demonic covenants existing, the covenants can be used as a breach to launch an assault on them. It's vitally important to pray concerning any hidden covenants so you can address them directly.

Are you aware that when a person comes for prayer on behalf of someone else (in proxy) they are the "point of contact" for the person in need of prayer? They stand in the gap for the person who is not there physically. When the enemy is using a person, the person can become the point of contact opening breaches reckoning havoc in the lives of those they are connected to. Take for example, if a person moved into your home that is financially cursed and you were sharing expenses; their continuous financial issues will affect the arrangement. It will cause you to chokingly take up their slack. The person under the curse may not see or recognize what is going on, and may not realize you are carrying most of the responsibility; because the god of this world blinds them. When you carry the burdens that belong to someone else you are taking the weight of it (burden) unto yourself. This is called carrying someone else's load.

Likewise, many people are carrying evil loads in the spirit realm unknown to them. Having revelation on the matter will free you from evil burdens. An evil load can be an arrow of sickness, poverty, or failure, etc. An older gentleman once told me that he did a ritual to bring harm to a woman in order to move her out of her position at work. He wanted his wife to have the position. Unknown to the woman she became accident-prone and injured herself nearly to the point of death. Although, he stated he became frighten because he was not trying to cause her loss of life, she became his victim. As a consequence, this woman, being out of the position at work had to deal with her injuries, loss of income and possibly a reassignment if someone else is now in her position. Most companies will fill a position based on the company's needs and will not hold a position indefinitely.

When someone is practicing witchcraft they send evil loads to their potential victims. If the person who is being attacked has been barricaded with fire (prayer) the evil devices of the enemy "will not" work. I once had a dream in which someone was sending a heavy load to me by means of witchcraft. I saw an orange cat, whose leg was tangled up in a loaded cart; I gave the cart a push and sent it on its way back to the sender. If I had received the cart and started looking through it, it might have brought unnecessary burdens into my life. Dreams such as these are revealed for a reason, so that we may know what is being schemed, in the spirit realm against us.

This is particularly true when many are on the verge of a breakthrough, and something comes up in a dream, which cancels the blessings they were praying for, and expecting. Imagine failure at the edge of breakthrough! These are the selfish devices of the enemy against those who are unsuspecting of what is being planned against them in the spirit.

Accursed things

Another deceptive factor, which satan uses to infiltrate people's lives, is through accursed things. These accursed things (some of which are subtle and appear innocent) are clothing, coins, furniture, pictures, jewelry and so on, when they are dedicated to the Kingdom of Darkness. Although some of these accursed things are subtly passed on to many people, we should know they are detestable items and have discernment to know the difference. Don't second-guess yourself; it should not be handled. They (accursed items) carry a false demonic anointing that will open the door to evil spirits. You can try to rebuke, bind and cast out, but when the items are accursed ~ it only make sense to detach yourself from them. In other words, if you allow the accursed thing to remain, legally the evil spirits attached to it will remain.

When the door is closed, evil spirits will no longer have a right to dwell (they will be trespassers and can be legally evicted). If we have accursed things in our home there are demons attached to them.

You may wonder what is the correlation between accursed things and dreams, but there are many who experience strange visitations because of something in their homes. A person's atmosphere can have an influence on his/her dream life. This is why Christians should dedicate their possessions to God to honor him and to receive His Blessings. Joshua 7:13 admonishes us to get "up, sanctify (set apart for a holy purpose) the people, and say, sanctify yourselves for tomorrow; for thus says the Lord, the God of Israel: There are accursed things in the midst of you, O Israel. You cannot stand before your enemies until you take away from among the things devoted [to destruction].

Those in the kingdom of darkness dedicate their objects and material properties to satan, so their possessions become accursed and by extension those who come in contact with them. The Bible tells us that accursed things should be destroyed. Joshua 7:12 cautions as to why the Israelites could not stand before their enemies, but fled before them! The items were accursed and objects of destruction. You can't close the door completely without destroying and renouncing the handling of such objects. Many people skip over the renouncing and breaking covenant steps. Many have spent countless hours praying without breaking covenants therefore; they are putting the cart before the horse. They also do not break the soul ties and find themselves still connected spiritually. An invisible line is still attached to them wherever they go. God warns us, that He will cease to be with us unless we destroy the accursed things among us. It's vitally important to obtain knowledge to ensure we are not openly participating in the things that's an abomination to God. It's a matter of simply reading the Bible and gaining understanding of what God Hates.

My people are destroyed for lack of knowledge: because thou hast rejected knowledge, I will also reject thee, that thou shalt be no priest to me: seeing thou hast forgotten the law of thy God, I will also forget thy children. (Hosea 4:6)

Yes, "My people" is referring to God's people.

Don't be like His people who lack knowledge and suffer as a result. There's no one way the devil can try to manipulate God's people, he also does it through a practice I call evil tokens. This happens when demonic agents use coins as a point of contact. These coins are used to cipher finances and good health away, making them accursed items. Yes, inanimate objects can fight against you too, (a cursed object) even subtle ornaments like statues, objects given as gifts, or religious paraphernalia. You have to be spiritually discerning, and those who can "see" in the spirit realm; God will allow you to see what's taking place. We need discernment. There is a solution for those who have an ear to hear, what the Spirit of the Lord is saying. In other words, coins too can be accursed when demonic agents pray over them and many people have them stored in a piggy bank or just lying around their house; that's why it's important not to pick up coins laying around on the street. Many are suffering financially because they mingle these accursed items with their possessions.

Concerning Pets:

Believe it or not, even your family pets can be manipulated against you and become a point of contact for the enemy. If you have animals such as a cat or dog (not just limited to these animals) you will need to pray serious prayers over them to protect them from bewitchment. I personally allowed my daughter to get a small dog. I personally became attached to him. Ironically, he belonged to my daughter, but he was always around me, watching my every move following me everywhere I went. During my travel I had to leave the dog with several families to care for him. Upon returning, after increased levels of fasting and prayer, the dog was screeching and running from me in his cage wildly. He had to be calmed down, I knew evil spirits had invaded him and it was quite dramatic. After casting out evil spirits, the dog vomited and then he seemed all right. One day, I started calling serious prayers over the dog and dealing with any bewitchments as a precautionary, the dog started bleeding profusely. At first, we were trying to figure out where all this blood was coming from, I've never experienced this with him before. It appeared that he would not make it past 24 hours. It was during this time I put anointing oil in his water to drink, he recovered.

One night I had a night vision, the dog was coming back home sneaking back in through the balcony. The dog travelled from the balcony, passed my bed, heading to his cage and was about have a bowel movement in front of my bed. I jumped up out of the bed, to interrupt him. I realized that God had allowed me to see spiritually; the dog was going out at night. He (the dog) was being summons. The dog was being bewitched to fight against me. After explaining to my daughter the dog must leave our home, I got rid of the dog. If you find yourself with demonic animals (such as snakes, lizards, scorpions and frogs etc.) do not deceive yourself by praying over these types of animals. The solution is to get them out of your house and repent. These types of animals are points of contact and have evil powers attached to them.

Deliverance and house cleaning (spiritually and naturally) is what closes the doors to constant nightmares and evil night visitations. Many times conducting a house cleaning to rid yourself of destructive items in your house will clean up the spiritual atmosphere.

Un-confessed sins

Many Christians are dealing with the un-confessed sins of their families or the secret sins not permitted to be discussed. For example, many people have dabbled in witchcraft or participated in witchcraft. (You would be surprised to know how many will say they are Christians and they have participated in abominable acts). Furthermore, we may not know all of the sins our ancestors participated in; as a result, we need to renounce the wicked practices and truly repent for those who practiced witchcraft in our family line.

I am no longer surprised to find those professing to be Christians adopting practices from the kingdom of darkness. I have talked to many individuals who say they are Christians, yet they visit psychics. Many Christians are lighting candles for money, love, and health. These are practices from the kingdom of darkness. We must never forget that God is always watching what we do in secret.

When you enter the land the Lord your God is giving you, you must avoid the abhorrent practices of heathen nations. There must never be found among you anyone who sacrifices his son or daughter in the fire, anyone who practices divination, an omen reader, a soothsayer, a sorcerer, one who casts spells, and one who conjures up spirits, a practitioner of the occult, or a necromancer. Whoever does those things is repugnant to the Lord, instead the Lord your God is willing to drive these detestable things out from before you. You must be blameless before the Lord your God. Those nations who are about to be dispossessed and listen to omen readers and diviners, the Lord your God has not given you permission to do such things. Deut. 8:9-14.

Let's take the time to repent and ask God to have mercy upon us, our families and ancestors. We need to especially repent for any sins pertaining to polygamy (the spirit of polygamy is having more than one mate. We can pretend this is for people in other countries that practice polygamy, but it is the same spirit of sleeping around, having boyfriends after boyfriends or girlfriends after girlfriends), shedding of innocent blood and sexual perversions. If you stay prayerful, the Holy Spirit will bring to your memory other forgotten un-confessed sins that you also need to include.

Now, if you are wondering what all of this have to do with dreams let me briefly explain. I will discuss spirit husbands and spirit wives which visit men and women in their dreams in greater detail in another chapter. The spirit husbands and spirit wives are the spirits that have sexual intercourse with people while they sleep. Also, take note if you are to be engaged, or you are offered dowry, having sexual relations and presented with gifts in your dreams you are dealing with this spirit.

Dream: I was walking past a condo type building and heard a discussion pertaining to myself. I knew it was about me although I did not know who was speaking. There was a dowry that was offered in the amount of $10,000 to marry me in 10 days. I thought how could someone be negotiating my marital life and who was this person?

Action: This was very strange to me that a spiritual marriage was being arranged without my permission. I immediately prayed dangerous prayers against "spirit husband" and extended my current 10-day fast to an additional 10 days.

Results: After intense prayers against the "spirit husband" I sat down on my bed and received deliverance that night. I witnessed an evil spirit come out of my body (visibly) and I was set free. The reason I'm sharing this information with you is to bring awareness. Well, you can live a life of being free from any evil spirit because of the Blood of Jesus. If you are having dreams and receiving evil loads; evil plantations; or having sex in your dreams; there are spiritual issues you need to deal with.

Now, you must be proactive and cancel your negative dreams and paralyze the works of dream invaders EVERY day.
I want you to understand that you cannot break free if you are not transparent, especially with yourself.

Dream invaders conduct initiations through dreams and witchcraft feeding. If you have dreams of eating various foods and meats in your sleep you must pray serious prayers to cancel and uproot what has been planted. Eating foods in your dreams allow demonic agents to manipulate and feed you spiritually in your sleep. If you have such dreams, when you awake pray the following prayer points. (Note: sometimes a person may not remember they have such dream. It's best to pray the prayers anyway, there no such thing as a wasted prayer.

Prayer point:

* Do not be alarmed if you have to vomit after repeating the 1st prayer point below.

I command every evil plantation in my life, to come out with all your roots, in the name of Jesus. (Lay your hands on your stomach and keep repeating).

I bind all the activities of demonic manipulations in my dreams and visions, in the name of Jesus.

I reject every evil spiritual load placed on me through dreams, in the name of Jesus.

I cancel all visions, dreams, evil words and curses against my progress, in the name of Jesus.

I expel from my body every strange material, in Jesus name.
Spiritual Training

Many churches have already been infiltrated by witches and warlocks (demonic agents) who are on assignment to ensure that no attention is given to prayer; wreak havoc and create division among the brethren. How many intercessors, prayer warriors, watchmen, prophets and teachers have been run off because they were sounding the alarm?

The Church should be well past "basic" training at this stage and onto "advance" training. Fighting the enemy in your dream life requires you to be diligent in prayer and in the reading of the Word of God. The enemy tries to take advantage by fighting Christians during their sleep; attempting to come and go undetected.

Most Christians are not aware that during their sleep it's when those who practice witchcraft are pronouncing curses. Most Christians go to sleep too early and get up too late to cancel anything. Their (Christians) day is already set in motion. It is during the nighttime that demonic agents are attempting to project into people's homes and launching their attacks. Normally, when a person receives wisdom on how to handle the astral projection, it dissipates. Those who understand what the enemy is doing and who pray during the night have a greater advantage than those who do not pray at all. After dreaming it is important to cancel demonic dreams to paralyze the works of the enemy against your life.

I'm concern that many people do not remember if they had a dream, or maybe some do not dream at all. They begin to see that they are not experiencing a victorious life: suffering financial losses, unexplainable sicknesses, and family problems. Many people would never suspect that their issues came from their dreams being manipulated.

As a result, the Church needs to prepare and train their members on how to fight spiritual battles; it must be done with more than a few selected Christians who are prepared for combat. There has to be more than a few faithful Christians who are on the front line. It's a shame that most Christians have to learn how to fight at home instead at Church. Although, this fight does prepare the Christian for battle, soldiers must be taught how to use their weapons. The Church has to step up to the plate.

Scriptures

"Be strong in the Lord and in the power of His might. Put on the whole armor of God that you may be able to stand against the wiles of the devil. For we do not wrestle against flesh and blood, but against principalities, against powers, against the rulers of the darkness of this age, against spiritual hosts of wickedness in the heavenly places.

"Therefore take up the whole armor of God that you may be able to withstand in the evil day, and having done all, to stand. Stand therefore, having girded your waist with truth, having put on the breastplate of righteousness, and having shod your feet with the preparation of the gospel of peace; above all, taking the shield of faith with which you will be able to quench all the fiery darts of the wicked one. And take the helmet of salvation, and the sword of the Spirit, which is the word of God; praying always with all prayer and supplication in the Spirit, being watchful to this end with all perseverance and supplication for all the saints...." (Ephesian 6:10-18)

"Beloved, do not believe every spirit, but test the spirits, whether they are of God; because many false prophets have gone out into the world" 1 John 4:1

"For though we walk in the flesh, we do not war according to the flesh. For the weapons of our warfare are not carnal but mighty in God for pulling down strongholds, casting down arguments and every high thing that exalts itself against the knowledge of God, bringing every thought into captivity to the obedience of Christ, and being ready to punish all disobedience when your obedience is fulfilled." 2 Corinthians 10:2-6

"Do not be discouraged because of this vast army. For the battle is not yours, but God's." 2 Chronicles 20:15

"Behold, I send you out as sheep in the midst of wolves. Therefore be wise as serpents and harmless as doves.

When they deliver you up, do not worry about how or what you should speak. For it will be given to you in that hour what you should speak; for it is not you who speak, but the Spirit of your Father who speaks in you." Matthew 10:16, 19-20

"And they overcame him by the blood of the Lamb and by the word of their testimony." Revelation 12:11

"Be ready in season and out of season. Convince, rebuke, exhort, with all long suffering and teaching. For the time will come when they will not endure sound doctrine, but according to their own desires, because they have itching ears, they will heap up for themselves teachers; and they will turn their ears away from the truth, and be turned aside to fables. But you be watchful in all things..."
2 Timothy 4:2-5

"Rejoice always, pray without ceasing, in everything give thanks; for this is the will of God in Christ Jesus for you. Do not quench the Spirit. Do not despise prophecies. Test all things; hold fast what is good. Abstain from every form of evil." 1 Thessalonians 5:16-22

And they shall fight against thee; but they shall not prevail against thee; for I am with thee, saith the LORD, to deliver thee. 1 Jer. 1:9

Wherefore thus saith the LORD God of hosts, Because ye speak this word, behold, I will make my words in thy mouth fire, and this people wood, and it shall devour them. Jer. 5:14

GOD SPEAKS

God speaks to us in dreams to give warnings, understanding, and counsel. I will bless the Lord who has counseled me; indeed, my mind (inner man) instructs me in the night. (Ps. 16:7 NASB)

There are many who do not believe God still speaks to his people through dreams. However, The Bible states that God will pour out His Spirit upon all flesh. Those of us open to God speaking to us will receive divine revelations and instructions. If you reject dreams and visions from God you are hindering the counsel of the Almighty Supreme God: God of Abraham, Isaac and Jacob (Israel).

And it shall come to pass in the last days," saith God, "I will pour out of My Spirit upon all flesh: and your sons and your daughters shall prophesy, and your young men shall see visions, and your old men shall dream dreams (Acts 2:17).

The significant is not just that God will allow men and women to have dreams, they will be able to "prophesy" and "see visions" with these dreams. Let's take Solomon for example, he asked God for wisdom and understanding and it was granted. Interestingly enough, the request was made to Solomon in a dream. God asked him what he wanted. Let's take a look at the conversation that took place in the dream. In Gibeon the LORD appeared to Solomon in a dream by night: and God said:

(God said to Solomon) Ask what I shall give thee. (Solomon said) give therefore thy servant an understanding heart to judge Thy people that I may discern between good and bad: for who is able to judge this Thy so great a people? Behold, I have done according to thy words: lo, I have given thee a wise and an understanding heart; so that there was none like thee before thee, neither after thee shall any arise like unto thee.... And Solomon awoke; and, behold, it was a dream (I Kings 3:5,9,12,15).

Could it be that you may have been given the solution to your problem in a dream already? Could it be that the instructions you need is already locked up inside of you? Could it be that God is allowing you to see, what the enemy is planning against you so that you can cancel, neutralize, and paralyze its effect?

For God speaketh once, yea twice, yet man perceive it not. In a dream, in a vision of the night, when deep sleep falleth upon men, in slumbering upon the bed; Then He openeth the ears of men, and sealeth their instruction, that He may withdraw man from his purpose, and hide pride from man. He keepeth back his soul from the pit, and his life from perishing by the sword (Job 33:14-18)

Without a doubt, recognizing and acting on your dreams should be as essential as eating. Dreams provide sustenance to ones overall well-being just as a balanced diet. If we do not open our "ear" and might I just add minds, then we can suffer unnecessary loss.

Dreams

It is important to pray for protection and barricade your valuable dream life. Your dreams are your spiritual monitors similar to watching a movie screen. Let me reiterate, dreams are one of the many ways God communicates with us. Dreams reveal your past and your future, and this is why we must pay attention to them. If you are having re-occurring dreams there is something that you need to address. God is trying to get your attention in the matter. I'm reminded of Samuel when the Lord was calling him, instructed by Eli to say "Speak Lord your servant is listening"

Spiritual Monitor

Dreams may have various meanings to different people, and this is why I strongly recommend that you pray before sharing your dreams. Spiritual monitors are like a bank camera recording those who enter the bank. In other words it provides surveillance for reviewing details at a later time. The meaning of dreams can vary and more revelation can be given over time for more clarity.

Dreams can be very detailed recording specific movements and actions you are to take note of. It's recommended that you keep a notepad, pen or recorder to document your dreams otherwise you could lose these critical parts of the dream that you need to remember. Upon waking if you vaguely remember having a dream, ask the Holy Spirit to bring it to your remembrance.

Furthermore, our spirit does not sleep and is active throughout the night. If YOU actively control your spirit in the night to go to places at your command, you are practicing witchcraft. This is called astral projection. This is what witches, warlocks and satanic agents do. When

God is directing, you are in safe hands. Anything done outside of the will of God is forbidden.

And he said to me:

Son of man, take all my words that I speak to you, to heart and listen carefully. Go to the exiles, to your fellow countrymen, and speak to them – say to them, 'This is what the sovereign Lord says,' whether they pay attention or not. Then a wind lifted me up and I heard a great rumbling sound behind me as the glory of the Lord rose from its place, and the sound of the living beings' wings brushing against each other, and the sound of the wheels alongside them, a great rumbling sound. A wind lifted me up and carried me away. I went bitterly, my spirit full of fury, and the hand of the Lord rested powerfully on me. I came to the exiles at Tel Abib, who lived by the Kebar River. I sat dumbfounded among them there, where they were living, for seven days. Ezekiel 3:10-15

If you used to dream and now you're no longer dreaming, your dream life has come under attack. Your dreams are the events of issues to be dealt with: the information God is trying to get to you and the surveillance camera revealing what the enemy is attempting to conjuring up against you. Again, upon waking cancel EVERY negative dream that you had through the night. It's more effective if you cancel them being specifically. Praying general blanket prayers may not hit the target in the bulls' eye. In fact, the general prayers may be praying amiss, hoping to hit anything moving against you. Learning how to recognize when the enemy is working against your dream life is important. Also, how to pray against the actual plans the enemy in plotting. The Holy Spirit will guide you to cancel and neutralize every scheme, from the kingdom of darkness. If you do not remember dreaming, cancel all negative dreams anyway it won't hurt. It is always better to be proactive because "prevention is better than the cure". When you develop the habit of canceling negative or demonic dreams you will begin to experience more breakthroughs in your life. You will find out that you were always on the verge of a breakthrough, but the enemy was stealing it from you before the manifestation. You shall receive your break through, in Jesus name,

Prayer Points:

Every negative dream I had through the night be neutralize by the Blood of Jesus, in Jesus Name. Amen.

Let every organized strategy of the host of the demonic world against my life be rendered useless, in the name of Jesus.

Your results in the natural indicate what has taken place in the spiritual realm.

Wrong Interpretations

Remember, that I already established earlier that people interpret dreams differently and that can be dangerous to the dreamer. The danger in receiving the wrong interpretation opens the door to confusion and delay. It also serves the enemy's purpose of diverting your destiny when God is directing or counseling you. God wants us to have a clear understanding of what He is communicating to us. I have found that people generally will allow anyone to interpret for them. Now, it is possible to have one person interpret a dream and another person can get additional information, which compliments. Dreams can be multifaceted, but we must be careful to use care when we reveal our dreams. When Joseph gave Pharaoh the interpretation in Gen. 41:25-32 He explained that the dream was repeated twice because God established it and God will shortly bring it to pass. Well the enemy can give recurring dreams for reinforcement, which has to be cancelled immediately. Recurring dreams must be given your undivided attention so you can take action.

My concern is that in desperation the dreamer may be led astray by not using discernment. The dreamer must pray concerning whom they will share their dreams with. It is during these vulnerable times that God may give us a recurring dream so that we do not miss what He (God) is saying. A recurring dream should be given immediate attention. It is important that the dream is recognized as a recurring and urgent message.

Dream Attacks

One of the purposes of this book is to shed light on dreams that we need to especially pay attention to like sexual dreams, dreams of being chased, shot, in the hospital, put into a cage, imprisoned, having animals attacking you or going back to your old high school, house or place of employment (job).

If you are eating with people that are deceased, and dreaming of having conversations with deceased family members you are dealing with ancestral powers or spirit of death. It's very important to deal with these types of dreams, to prevent evil carryover or sickness. These types of dreams show a soul-tie and/or covenants are still in place, which must be broken. Ancestral powers also attack those who have left their family's religion, giving their life to Jesus. Those who are being pursued by the spirit of death have dreams of accidents, injuries or being pursued by spiritual assassinators.

Some individuals have been dedicated to family idols and now they are being pursued by ancestral powers to return back. Also, if everyone in your family had certain limitations and you break free it is like the powers are screaming "WHO DO YOU THINK YOU ARE?" The Powers are upset that you are now free. If your ancestors were poverty stricken, that's not your lot! You need to open your mouth and declare, "Poverty is not my lot", in Jesus name.

In addition, many people talk with dead family members openly to receive information or direction. I have personally counseled people who either dream or see apparitions and sought information or direction from those who were deceased. This practice is forbidden.

The bible tells us that (in Deut.18:9) when you enter the land the Lord your God is giving you, you must not learn the abhorrent practices of those nations. There must never be found among you anyone who sacrifices his son or daughter in the fire, anyone who practices divination, an omen reader, a soothsayer, a sorcerer, one who casts spells, one who conjures up spirits, a practitioner of the occult, or a necromancer.

Whoever does these things is abhorrent to the Lord and because of these detestable things the Lord your God is about to drive them out from before you. You must be blameless before the Lord your God. Those nations that you are about to dispossess listen to omen readers and diviners, but the Lord your God has not given you permission to do such things.

Dreams of Vehicles

If you have a dream of being in a vehicle and you are losing control of the vehicle heading for a crash, pray and cancel all accidents. If someone else is driving pray to unseat every evil driver. There are eaters of flesh and drinkers of blood who prey on people setting up car accidents. Shall the prey be taken from the mighty, or the lawful captive delivered?

But thus saith the LORD, Even the captives of the mighty shall be taken away, and the prey of the terrible shall be delivered: for I will contend with him that contendeth with thee, and I will save thy children. And I will feed them that oppress thee with their own flesh; and they shall be drunken with their own blood, as with sweet wine: and all flesh shall know that I the LORD am thy Saviour and thy Redeemer, the mighty One of Jacob. Is 49:24-26

Mountain of Fire and Miracle Ministries (MFM) church in Lagos, Nigeria had an experience where a man admitted after giving his life to Christ, that he played a part in trying to kill a Christian man. He admitted that there was a Christian that they were trying to kill and they set up numerous accidents for him, but they failed at every attempt. They set up an accident involving a bus and everyone died except the Christian man they were after. The people trying to kill the Christian were "eaters of flesh and drinkers of blood" This practice is used by those use enchantments trying to causes accidents and deaths. Here is what the Lord says He will do to them "And I will feed them that oppress thee with their own flesh; and they shall be drunken with their own blood, as with sweet wine: and all flesh shall know that I the LORD am thy Saviour and thy Redeemer, the mighty One of Jacob. Is 49:26

I have always heard that "your ministry" is a vehicle. If a person dreams that they lose control of a vehicle, it does not necessarily mean that their ministry is out of control. However one should not sit back and wonder what will happen if I do not pray for protection and cancel the dream?

Whosoever diggeth a pit shall fall therein: and he that rolleth a stone, it will return upon him. Proverbs 26:27

Prayer Points:

Eaters of flesh and drinkers of blood, I am not your candidate fall into your own pit, in Jesus name. Amen.

Let all drinkers of blood and eaters of flesh turn upon themselves in the name of Jesus.

Blood of Jesus, restore my confused dreams to transparency in, Jesus name. Amen.

Familiar spirits

Familiar spirits operate in dreams, many of us are known quite well to familiar spirits because they monitor our actions and gather information to deceive. They distort personalities to perform their operations such as providing demonic information to manipulate.

Many churches invite speakers or prophets that operated under a familiar spirit. The prophets (false) prophesy to many through a familiar spirit that seemingly establishes them as prophets of God. They pervert the authentic prophetic ministry. Familiar spirits can cause much confusion in churches:

And it came to pass, as we went to prayer, a certain damsel possessed with a spirit of divination met us, which brought her masters much gain by soothsaying: The same followed Paul and us, and cried, saying, These men are the servants of the most high God, which shew unto us the way of salvation. And this did she many days. But Paul, being grieved, turned and said to the spirit, I command thee in the name of Jesus Christ to come out of her. And he came out the same hour. Acts 16:16-18 (KJV)

Although, the statement was a true statement the damsel operating under the spirit of divination was attempting to build creditability to influence others once the (Apostles) left town. Paul was vexed and I thank God he dealt with the situation.

Many people have dreams in which familiar spirits influence them during their sleep providing them with false information. They can show your enemies as your friend and your close friends as enemies. These spirits monitor closely and report back to the kingdom of darkness. They attempt to destroy by taking the same information they have obtained from monitoring their potential victims. Pray and ask God to let you know the assignment they have against you. God will reveal it so that you will have the victory.

PRAYER POINTS:

Impersonating agents of darkness taking my close friends or relatives' images to deceive me, and bring harm to me through my dreams, collapse with the rock of ages, in Jesus' name.

I claim all the good things, which God has revealed to me through dreams. I reject all bad and satanic dreams in the name of Jesus.

(You are going to be specific here. Place your hand on your chest and talk to God specifically about the dreams, which need to be cancelled. Cancel it with all your strength; command the fire of God to burn it to ashes.)

O Lord, perform the necessary surgical operation in my life and change all that has gone wrong in the spirit world, in Jesus' name.

I reclaim all of the good things, which I have lost as a result of defeat, in Jesus name.

I arrest every spiritual attacker and paralyze their activities in my life, in the name of Jesus.

I retrieve my stolen virtues, goodness and blessings in Jesus' name.

Let all satanic manipulations through dreams be dissolved, in Jesus' name.

Let all arrows, gunshots, wounds, harassment, and opposition in my dreams return to its sender, in the name of Jesus.

I reject every evil spiritual load placed on me through dreams, in Jesus' name.

All spiritual animals (cats, dogs, snakes, and crocodiles) paraded against me, be chained and return to the sender(s) in the name of Jesus.

*ANY PROJECTION INTO AN ANIMAL SENT AGAINST ME IS TRAPPED IN THAT ANIMAL, YOU SHALL NOT RETURN BACK ALIVE, IN THE NAME OF JESUS.

Holy Ghost, purge my intestine and my blood from satanic foods and injections, in Jesus' name.

I loose myself from curses, hexes, spells, bewitchment and evil domination directed against me through dreams in the name of Jesus.

Let all satanic manipulations through dreams be dissolved in Jesus' name.

Every evil spiritual load of poverty placed on me, sender carry your own evil load in Jesus' name.

I reject every evil spiritual load of sickness placed on me through dreams in Jesus' name.

I reject every evil spiritual load of backwardness placed on me through dreams in Jesus' name.

I reject every evil spiritual load of oppression placed on me through dreams in Jesus' name.

Holy Ghost Fire, purge my intestine and my blood from satanic foods and injections. IF YOU HAVE EATEN

ANY SATANIC FOODS ASK GOD TO UPROOT IT AND VOMIT OUT.

I break every evil covenant and initiation through dreams in the name of Jesus.

I Break any evil soul ties and covenants between me and _____, in the name of Jesus.

Evil Dreams - Dr. D.K. Olukoya

* Drinking (Dirty) Water - The enemy is polluting your spiritual life and attempting to make you lukewarm.

*Crying - the enemy is planning hard times and tribulations for you.

* Barriers/Roadblocks preventing you from moving forwards - the enemy is trying to hinder your progress. The enemy is attempting to barricade you from getting to the next level or moving forward in life.

* Eating Meat - participating in witchcraft feeding. Initiations to become a witch, (known or unknown to you) you have been initiated into witchcraft and need to break covenants and uproot all evil seeds planted in your life through dreams.

* Force Fed - If your mouth is being forced open or you are being force-fed, the enemy is planting sickness and introducing Luke warmness into your life. Make sure you command any evil plantations to come out with all its roots, in Jesus' name. (Begin to cough it out).

* Difficulty going up a mountain - The enemy is introducing struggles and challenges into your life. (Climbing the rough side of the mountain)

* Traffic Jam - the enemy is slowing down your progress and using delay tactics & sluggishness. Pray against the spirit of the turtle (tortoise) and the slug.

*Feeding/breastfeeding a strange baby - the enemy is sucking the milk out of your life. (Spiritual children)

*Falling into a pit - the enemy is trying to bury you alive and cause you to stumble.

*Wind and whirlwind fighting against you - God is trying to tell you that there are troubles ahead to retard your progress. (Pray aggressively against this)

*Documents stolen in the dream - the enemy are trying to make those documents worthless.

*Clothes stolen or missing - this is an attack on your honor, glory and virtue. You must recover it back (cover it in the Blood of Jesus) or command it to catch fire, in Jesus name.

*Bearing a heavy load - the enemy is trying to introduce burden bearing problems into your life.

*Retesting-continually sitting for examinations without finishing them - this is the spirit of frustration and failure (The Circle of failure.)

*Darkness in the dream - this represents spiritual blindness.

*Fire destroying things - the enemy is trying to introduce calamity and woe into your life. You have to pray violently.

*Traveling on a never ending road-the enemy is trying to introduce frustration into your life. Attempting to make reaching your destiny unattainable.

*Being shot, either with arrow or gun - the enemy is trying to introduce afflictions of a terrible kind into your life. Spiritual assassins assigned against you.

* Wearing rags - The spirit of poverty and lack.

Daniel -The Dream Interpreter

Daniel 2:23 say, "O God of my fathers, I acknowledge and glorify you, for you have bestowed wisdom and power on me. Now you have enabled me to understand what I requested from you. For you have enabled me to understand the king's dilemma."

Are you facing a dilemma and are looking for the solution? Well, if you are looking to God, He has the solution. You need wisdom from your Heavenly Father to enable you to comprehend what is needed for a successful outcome. Only God can bestow the wisdom and power needed for you to move forward, whether through dreams or night visions.

The Book of Daniel acknowledges that God reveals the deep and secret things. When you need to understand your dreams God will enable you to have understanding. Let's take for example the king who was facing a dilemma; and Daniel along with Shadrach, Meshach and Abednego sought God's favor. When Daniel approached the King, he did not take credit, he declared that God in Heaven, who reveals mysteries wanted to show the King what would happen in the days to come. Interestingly, Daniel received insight to not only tell the interpretation, but to rehash the actual dream that the King had forgotten.

He revealeth the deep and secret things: he knoweth what is in the darkness, and the light dwelleth with him. Daniel 2:22

Prayer point:

O God, give me the wisdom and power to take me to the level, where I'm supposed to be, in Jesus' name.

Fire of God; unseat every enemy sitting on my blessings, in the name of Jesus.

Open Doors

Prov. 26:2 As the bird by wandering, as the swallow by flying, so the curse causeless shall not come.

The bible tells us that a causeless curse shall not come, but if we are operating under a curse it's because of an opened door in our life (evil soul tie/evil covenant). You must ask the Lord to reveal anything that is hidden. A curse can operate because of many reasons, such as known or unknown sins. There may be something that you participated in knowingly or unknowingly that is affecting you, regardless of how long ago. In addition, we must seek God concerning the unknown doors that are opened in our lives.

Curses can also operate through family lines (ancestors), through evil practices or curses people pronounced upon themselves and their generations.

The bible gives us an illustration in which foolish men made statements against Apostle Paul, which became snares unto them.

But do not yield to their persuasion, for more than forty of their men are lying in ambush waiting for him, having bound themselves by an oath and under a curse neither to eat nor drink till they have killed him; and even now they are all ready, [just] waiting for your promise. Acts 23:21

Those who hate God and practicing idolatry place their future generation under a curse. This is where many find themselves, trying to figure out why life is a constant battle with much resistance. Could it be that someone in their family line is responsible for the curse? What is the possibility that there is an unchallenged curses lingering? Break it; Break it, in Jesus name.

Here is a scripture that tells us that if anyone bows down and turns against God to serve idols that they fall under a curse:

You shall not bow down yourself to them or serve them; for I the Lord your God am a jealous God, visiting the iniquity of the fathers upon the children to the third and fourth generation of those who hate Me. Ex 20:5 (AMP).

Let us thank the Lord for his grace and mercy.

Keeping mercy and loving kindness for thousands, forgiving iniquity and transgression and sin, but Who will by, NO MEANS clear the guilty, visiting the iniquity of the fathers upon the children and the children's children, to the third and fourth generation. Ex 34:7 (AMP).

When you have dreams that do not make sense, or appear to be disjointed (such as strange people committing vile acts around you) as a precaution you should repent. You must ask God to forgive any unconfessed or un-repented sin committed by you or anyone in your family.

There are sins you or members of your family may have committed or overlooked (sins never dealt with). Once you form the habit of going before God with a repentance heart then it is time to deal with the curse, you will witness the difference it makes in your life, once you begin dealing with these curses hanging over your head. It will definitely be a burden lifted, in Jesus name.

There are also further steps that you must take such as breaking evil covenants formed. Once you have broken the covenants/curses, and then deal with the demons assigned to those curses. Ask the Lord where you should send them, or send them to the pit of hell until the day of judgment. If you need further assistance pray for divine direction as to who could walk you through the deliverance process. Although all ministries should deal with deliverance, many are deliverance ministries only by name, and not by power. It is important to undergo counseling and deliverance. Deliverance ministers should undergo deliverance frequently themselves, cleansing themselves from evil plantations.

Many people live their lives having cycles of accidents, spiritual attacks in which they experience defeat (in and out of hospitals, suffering frequent financial losses) all because they have not addressed the unbroken curses that are hanging over their heads. It's like the clichéd dark cloud following them everywhere they go. Many Christians undergo much warfare defeats simply because they are in need of deliverance. Most of the time you will hear Christians say it because of their anointing. Yes, it could be sometimes, but Jesus was anointed and in all his attacks He had the victory. You cannot go into the enemy's camp to declare war, when you are still sleeping with the enemy. I have seen personally more than enough of those who say they are Christians but they are smoking, drinking, lustful; and it's enough to make a babe in Christ confused! One thing for sure is that the devil knows who is playing and who is not.

Prayer point:

Every dark cloud over my head, scatter; in Jesus' name.

Dreams of Demotion

Many people have dreams of demotion and because they do not recognize their dreams as such, they allow the dreams to remain unchallenged.

I once had someone tell me they had recurring dreams in which they were back at their past high school retaking exams. This is the spirit of retrogression. This person currently is unable to move forward, experiencing roadblocks in education, employment, housing, transportation and so on. Have you ever heard of the saying "one step forward and two steps back"?

You should not be dreaming of retaking a test back at your past high school. It is an indication that the power of retrogression is working in your life. Why would you be dreaming about going back 2, 5, 10, or 20 years ago; undergoing an examination that you have passed already in the natural realm?

Now some dream interpretation books would say you are perhaps undergoing a test, but you passed the test in the natural, you graduated. The enemy is trying to set you back. You have to reject these types of dreams. You already graduated from high school! Many people have dreams of demotion and wonder why they are not moving forward in academics, employment, financially, or in business.

Prayer Points:

Every power of backwardness operating in any area of my life, fall down and die, in Jesus name.

Every dream of demotion halt, in the name of Jesus.

Every Power attempting to demote me I am not your candidate, die, in Jesus' name.

If we have a teachable spirit and seek God's face we will begin to see his manifold blessings in our lives. There are those who practice abominable acts during the night to destroy destinies and to accomplish the wicked works of the devil. You must be able to see the evil devices fashioned against you. If only you knew the many people who profess to be Christian, who work witchcraft against fellow Christians.

Prayer points:
Every power planting affliction into my life through dreams, be buried alive in the name of Jesus.

Oh God, My Father, open my eyes so that I can clearly see, in Jesus Name.

We must pray and ask God to help us interpret our dreams. If you have many dreams and do not understand them, you must cry out to God. It's not God's desire to speak to you through dreams and leave you, without understanding the message. It is not His desire for you to have to ask someone everyday to interpret your dreams. You should at least have a general knowledge of what the dream is saying, and there should be confirmation of the interpretation. Now, let me say this: we must make sure we do not deceive ourselves, trying to make the dream say what we want it to say. It's sad when someone has an idol in their heart and they do not want a correct interpretation. I've seen this when a person is believing someone is their husband/wife because of a dream, when its really because the person has become an idol in their heart. It was not a dream from God, and they cannot be convinced otherwise.

Prayer point:
Heavenly father, sharpen my spiritual vision and increase my discernment, in Jesus name.

The Cup Bearer's and The Baker's Dream

The cupbearer and the baker both had a dream the same night. When the baker was given the interpretation in three days "he would be hung on a tree and the birds shall eat thy flesh from off thee". There is no indication that he cried out for mercy, for a reversal. It was a destiny-destroying dream.

In Gen. 40:5, The cupbearer and the baker of the king of Egypt, who were confined in the prison, both had a dream the same night. Each man's dream had its own meaning. Gen. 40:8 further indicates that they told him (Joseph): "[w]e both had dreams, but there is no one to interpret them." Joseph responded, "[d]on't interpretations belong to God? Tell them to me."

I want to focus only on the interpretation of the dream. According to Gen. 40:12 "[t]his is its meaning," Joseph said to them. "The three branches represent three days." Some dreams will tell you the timing associated with them. It imperative that you cancel and reverse every demonic dream immediately after waking. We should not take it for granted that we have more time than we actually do.

Many people have recorded their dreams and filed it away for years; they were supposed to cancel many of them. Many of the un-canceled dreams have already come to pass because they were uncontested. There are many broken marriages, lost businesses, sicknesses, and diverted destinies because prompt action was not taken.

Let's take a look at some of the numbers mentioned in the following dreams:

Likewise, the cupbearer's dream of three branches stood for three days (Gen. 39:12), and for the chief baker, the three baskets represented three days (Gen. 39:18). In Pharaoh's dream, the seven cows were seven years (Gen. 41:26).

Let us look at the significance of numbers in dreams. When Joseph dreamed of eleven stars, the eleven was literal, but the stars were symbolic and actually represented his brothers. Joseph was dreaming about his eleven brothers (Gen. 37:1-11). Likewise, the cupbearer's dream of three branches represented three days (Gen. 39:12), and for the chief baker, the three baskets represented three days (Gen. 39:18). In Pharaoh's dream, the seven cows were seven years (Gen. 41:26). So we can expect numbers to mean that exact number of something.

Although people may have similar dreams, we must remember that dreams can represent something entirely different to the other person. In addition, the baker and the butler had dreams that were not identical, but quite similar. The baker assumed that his dream represented something good since the butler's dream was encouraging. There was a slight difference the birds were eating from his basket that indicated that he was going to be hung and the birds would eat his flesh.

You have to allow God to give the interpretation. When your dreams are being interpreted for you, you should also receive a confirmation from God.
We all have dreams at night (sometimes similar) but each person's dream has its own meaning.

Genesis 37:5 also highlights that Joseph had a dream, and when he told his brothers about it, they hated him even more. In other words, you must remember that you cannot share your dreams with everyone. We must use wisdom; there are dream assassins and destiny killers, who perform spiritual abortions on the unsuspecting. I call these individuals "evil midwives". Dreams of your destiny are important and you must not place them in the hands of the enemy (demonic agents) assigned to hinder or abort what God has for you.

There was a time when I asked someone (prophets online) to interpret my dream (I already knew the interpretation, but was seeking a seeming confirmation). The interpretation he gave was so far off and depressing. I also disagreed with the interpretation he was giving to other individuals who posted prior to me. So I quickly reposted the dream and a prophet who I discerned was in tune to hearing God was selected to interpret it. I waited eagerly for the answer. The interpretation was perfect. I'm giving this example to show the importance of discerning who to share your dreams with. I'm currently watching the prophecy come to pass. You have to watch out for the dream killers; they're out there.

Witchcraft Power

"Therefore thus saith the Lord GOD; behold, I am against your pillows, wherewith ye there hunt the souls to make them fly, and I will tear them from your arms, and will let

the souls go, even the souls that ye hunt to make them fly."
Ezek 13:20

While some are sleeping they have felt their spirits leaving their bodies. I know of someone who while sleeping their spirit was summons. The plot of the enemy was to summons her spirit to a witchcraft coven to deal with her because of her ministry work. It was the saving grace of God and His protection that the enemy's plan was foiled. She realized that she needed to pray prayers with fire for protection.

If you are conducting spiritual warfare you should pray prayers of protection over yourself and your family before going to sleep. Prayers that will paralyze the operations of the enemy: to stop your enemies in their tracks. I'm reminded of a short time ago when we received a phone call into the ministry. A young woman stated that her mother would ask her to check on her from time to time, to see if she was still breathing; while she covered her face with a handkerchief lying in the bed. Her mother was a witch who was allowing her spirit to travel on demonic assignments. Her daughter was wondering why their household was being bombarded with spiritual attacks. Actually, many people know the answer to their dilemma; her mother and the other witches were fighting among themselves to gain more power. Many people ask for prayers on their behalf, but they are still actively involved with the occult. This person (her mother) was projecting her spirit for witchcraft purposes. How can a person do the work of the devil and asked the Christians to help out? The devil is a deceiver. Let us thank God our Heavenly Father for discernment.

It is important to make sure you are protected. I cannot stress the importance. Again, if you are conducting spiritual warfare you should pray prayers of protections over yourself and your family before going to sleep. You need to make sure you cover yourself after speaking with people on the phone, prior to lying down. Prayers that will paralyze the enemies operations, to backfire every arrow sent your way.

No weapon that is formed against us shall prosper and every tongue, which rises against us in judgment, we do condemn. This is our heritage as servants of the Lord and our righteousness is from You, O Lord of Hosts.

Dreaming is definitely one way God speaks to us, providing us with information, directions, and warnings. The dreams we dream also show what is being designed for us in the spiritual realm. If you are a person who does not take your dreams seriously or does not remember your dreams, an evil exchange could be taking place. An example of an evil exchange is when you are spending money in the spirit realm or giving away your money, trading your wealth for poverty. It is when something good is being stolen from you and replaced with something evil.

Dream:

I was in a small office setting and my son was handing out regular sized envelopes. Included in the envelopes was money. As the recipients started opening the envelopes they were given, I realized my money was being given away. I started going to each person to recover the envelopes before the rest of the people could open theirs. I was collecting my money just as fast as my son was handing it out. Upon waking I cancelled the dream, which could have led to devastating financial problems. The dream reflected my money being wasted, given away, and depleted. Notice, it was my son, basically giving it (my money) away. I had to cancel my son causing me financial hardship. I also know when I have certain types of dreams and start seeing negative things manifesting in my life, it is an indication of the areas in need of prayer.

Prayer Point:

I recover ALL of my money that was given away in the spirit realm, in Jesus Name.

My children will not be used by the enemy to give away or waste my money, in Jesus Name.

Matthew 13:25 says, that while men slept the enemy planted evil seed. Contrary to some beliefs, dreams do not represent the unconscious; dreams are the dark speech of the spirit. If you have dreams and you do not understand them now is the time to get knowledge. I want you to remember what I highlighted earlier; ignorance will not exempt you from the sneers of the devil!

Another parable put he forth unto them, saying, The kingdom of heaven is likened unto a man which sowed good seed in his field: But while men slept, his enemy came and sowed tares among the wheat, and went his way. But when the blade was sprung up, and brought forth fruit, then appeared the tares also. So the servants of the householder came and said unto him, Sir, didst not thou sow good seed in thy field? from whence then hath it tares? He said unto them, An enemy hath done this. The servants said unto him, Wilt thou then that we go and gather them up?

But he said, nay; lest while ye gather up the tares, ye root up also the wheat with them. Let both grow together until the harvest: and in the time of harvest I will say to the reapers, Gather ye together first the tares, and bind them in bundles to burn them: but gather the wheat into my barn. Matt 13:24-30

The bible tells us that while men slept, the enemy came and polluted their harvest by sowing tares among the wheat, and went his way. The evil seed was allowed to flourish, when the blade sprung up, fruit came forth. The good fruit was almost jeopardized because of the "tares". If one were to listen to this homophone, they might have thought that the bible was referring to "tears". And in some ironic way, those "tears" might have been the result of the "polluted harvest". Some scriptures are multi-references, meaning they can be applied to different situations.

The question may also be asked; did I not sow good seed? You might have sowed good seed, but at night while you were sleeping your harvest might have been tampered with. The servant said, should we go and gather up the tares, but he said, NO. When you gather the tares you will root up the wheat with them. Now, let them both grow together until harvest time. Since the enemy was not dealt with prior to the evil plantation, it would require additional effort to enjoy the harvest. A harvest that no doubt is malnourished since some of those tares sucked the nutrients from the soil, preventing your harvest from reaping the full benefits.

The wheat and tare must be separated now. It is now time for harvesting, it is now time to separate yourself from the turmoil created from letting "nature run its course". Lack of wisdom and understanding prevented the loss of the wheat. The evil plantation of the tares was an assignment to bring loss, defeat, and destruction at the edge of a breakthrough. The "tares" popped up so that they could hinder the wheat's growth just as the bible reveals to us "My people are destroyed for a lack of knowledge." Therefore you can be a prayer warrior, a worship leader or a Pastor of a large congregation and be defeated because of the dreams you failed to take action against. If God is willing to give you the keys to the Kingdom, He will give you the necessary keys to unlock the mysteries concerning your life.

Further, if you have ever experienced waking and felt worn out like you were in a fight, you need to take heed. If you wake up with a headache, pain under your ribs, scratches on your body or feeling as if someone was holding you down; it's time to fight back!

Prayer Point:

Every dream invader fighting against me in my sleep, fight against yourself and destroy yourself, in Jesus' name.

We need to praise God for speaking to us through dreams and leading us on the path to reach our destiny. We also need to thank God for allowing us to see the evil devices and manipulations of the enemies to set roadblocks before us. Now, that you are more sensitive to what takes place while you are sleeping, you will better equipped to deal with dream invaders.

We must bulldoze our way through these delayed tactics of the enemy to hinder us from fulfilling what God has commissioned us to do. We have the power to tread upon the serpents and scorpions. Luke 10:19 reminds us that "[b]ehold, I give unto you power to tread on serpents and scorpions, and over all the power of the enemy: and nothing shall by any means hurt you."

Dreams of Water

If you have a dream in which you are trying to find your way out of the forest, or walking in the river, ocean or sea, you may be going to witchcraft meetings in the marine kingdom. Marine witchcraft is very destructive and causes the most havoc in the lives of their victims.

And there came one of the seven angels which had the seven vials, and talked with me, saying unto me, Come hither; I will show unto thee the judgment of the great whore that sitteth upon many waters: with whom the kings of the earth have committed fornication, and the inhabitants of the earth have been made drunk with the wine of her fornication. Revelation 17: 1

Ezek 29:1-3 also tells us:

that in the tenth year, in the tenth mouth. In the twelfth day of the month, the word of the Lord came unto me, saying, son of man, set thy face against Pharaoh King of Egypt, and prophesy against him, and against all Egypt:

speak, and say, thus saith the Lord God; Behold, I am against thee, Pharaoh king of Egypt, the great dragon that lieth in the midst of his rivers, which hath said, my river is mine own, and I have made it for myself.

In the beginning, God created man to subdue the earth and have dominion over all of the flesh of the sea, and over the fowl of the air and over everything creature that moveth upon the face of the earth. If you are sailing in boats, working in the ocean, or walking in the ocean (waters), pray these prayers seriously. These are the powers that introduce the spirit husbands and spirit wives in dreams. The spirit husbands and spirit wives, used interchangeable with the incubi or succubus spirits, have sex with people while they are sleeping.

They also cause confusion in marriages and initiate fights between the spouses. The spirit husband and spirit wife's goal is to break up marriages so that they can have the spouse to themselves. They are always in competition with the other spouse. These spirits are violating spirits and need to be dealt with seriously. Consider a prayer and fasting program. How be it this kind goeth not out but by prayer and fasting. Matt 17:21 (KJV)

Prayer Point:

Any witchcraft practice under any water against my life, receive immediate judgment of fire, in the name of Jesus. Let every evil altar under water upon which certain evil is done against me roast, in the name of Jesus.

Every priest ministering at an evil altar against me inside any water, fall down and die, in the name of Jesus.

Any power under any river or sea remotely-controlling my life, be destroyed by fire, and I shake myself loose from your hold, in the name of Jesus.

Gideon's dream: Dreams to encourage you to move forward!!!

When Gideon arrived, he heard a man telling another man about a dream he had. The man said, "Look! I had a dream. I saw a stale cake of barley bread rolling into the

Midianite camp. It hit a tent so hard it knocked it over and turned it upside down. The tent just collapsed.

When Gideon heard the report of the dream and its interpretation, he praised God. Then he went back to the Israelite camp and said, 'Get up, for the Lord is handing the Midianite army over to you!' Jdg. 7:13 & 15

Upon Gideon's hearing about the report of the dream he took immediate action. The people of God were waiting for the command and once Gideon heard the report, He praised God. The scriptures explain that he went back to the camp and said "Get up". Now is the time, and victory was given to them, all they had to do was head for battle and God would do the rest. Yes, God delivered their enemies into their hands.

This illustration shows the need to pray for divine revelation and the revealing of dark secrets. If we are going to dream, we must cry out for the wisdom to interpret what we see.

Remember, the dream Joseph interpreted for the Butler and the Baker, a dream in which 3 days later they experienced the outcome. The bible does not indicate whether the baker prayed for the cancelation of the dream. However, when we examine some of the people in the bible receiving bad news, the cried out to God. After careful study we will see that some prayed and the God of mercy reverse the negative outcome.

Similarly, when Hezekiah was given a word from God to prepare his house he was going to die, Hezekiah cried out to God and God changed his outcome. Although, it was not a dream it shows God's is merciful.

In those days was Hezekiah sick unto death. And the prophet Isaiah the son of Amoz came to him and said unto him, Thus saith the LORD, Set thine house in order, for thou shalt die and not live.

Turn again and tell Hezekiah the captain of my people, Thus saith the LORD, the God of David thy father, I have heard thy prayer, I have seen thy tears, behold, I will heal thee: on the third day thou shalt go up unto the house of the LORD. II Kings 20:1

The bible shows us that when those who trust Him cry out to God, God in his mercy can reverse the outcome. Jonah also cried out and received a favorable outcome. While Jonah was in the fish belly he cried unto the Lord. Hear what Jonah said "They that observe lying vanities forsake their own mercy. But I will sacrifice unto thee with the voice of thanksgiving; I will pay that that I have vowed. Salvation is of the LORD." And the LORD spoke unto the fish, and it vomited out Jonah upon the dry land. Jonah 2:7-10. We have many examples of those who cried out to God and God heard them.

No Enchantment Against Jacob

God brought them out of Egypt; he hath as it were the strength of an unicorn. Surely there is no enchantment against Jacob, neither is there any divination against Israel: according to this time it shall be said of Jacob and of Israel, What hath God wrought! Number 23:22-23.

Do you remember the story about Balak who sent for Balaam to curse the children of Israel? The surrounding nations were afraid of the children of Israel because they heard about what Israel's God had done for them. Balak looked upon the children of Israel and said:

"Behold, there [are] a people come out from Egypt: behold, they cover the face of the earth, and they abide over against me." Balak told Balaam come, I need you to curse these people; for they are too mighty for me: peradventure I shall prevail, that we may smite them, and that I may drive them out of the land: for I wot?) that he whom thou blessest is blessed, and he whom thou cursest is cursed.

God visited Balaam and told him he was only permitted to say what God told him to say. And he (Balaam) took up his parable, and said, Rise up, Balak, and hear; hearken unto me, thou son of Zippor: God is not a man, that he should lie; neither the son of man, that he should repent:

hath he said, and shall he not do it? Or hath he spoken, and shall he not make it good?

Behold, I have received a commandment to bless: and he hath blessed; and I cannot reverse it. Num. 23:20

Do you understand what Balaam is saying here? If God blesses someone they are blessed. Let no man think he can reverse it. Balaam could not curse Jacob! Let us look at Numbers 23:21 He hath not beheld iniquity in Jacob, neither hath he seen perverseness in Israel: the LORD his God is with him, and the shout of a king is among them. If there are no open doors the curse will not have a landing place or entrance. Remember, the book of proverbs tells us that an undeserved curse will not work.

As the bird by wandering, as the swallow by flying, so the curse causeless shall not come. Proverbs 26:2. Many Christians are not aware they are being cursed; those who have a prayer life have a hedge of protection around them. As they (Christians) are carrying on with their day as usual, the curses have gone back to the sender simply, because the curse was without cause and they (Christians) were barricaded with fire (prayer).

No weapon that is formed against thee shall prosper; and every tongue that shall rise against thee in judgment thou shalt condemn. This is the heritage of the servants of the LORD, and their righteousness is of me, saith the LORD. Is 54:16-17

The time of the night when enchantments and casting spells take place is between 12 a.m.- 4 a.m. I once went into a Barnes and Noble bookstore late one night, a lady (witch) approached me to tell me that she went through an entire book and was looking for more books in the category of witchcraft.

When I took a closer look I realized that she was reading from a book of curses. She was possessed and blatantly determined to become more engrossed in darkness. She stated that she had read all 5000 curses and was looking for more. Matthew 13:25: But while men slept, his enemy came and sowed. It is during the night that evil people like this woman (witches) prey on those who are sleeping and with no fire (prayer).

PRAYER POINTS:

Edifying words of God overwhelm my dream life now in Jesus' name.

Every good dream I have ever received from God since I was born, manifest by fire in Jesus name.

Satanic manipulators of my dreams, receive the Angelic slap of death in Jesus' name.

I call out my body, soul, and spirit from demonic and witchcraft meetings in Jesus' name.

Every satanic number issued against me in a dream, I replace you with the promotional numbers of God, in Jesus' name.

Initiating witchcraft power, meet crushing angelic powers now and be destroyed by them, in Jesus' name.

Every sickness introduced into my life as a result of evil dreams; die, in the name of Jesus.

Every dream of past failures, die, in Jesus name.

Every witchcraft caterer feeding me in a dream, die, in Jesus' name.

Every satanic dream against my progress, die, in the name of Jesus.

Every dream of prison, release me, in the name of Jesus.

Every arrow of witchcraft fired into my dream, backfire, in Jesus name.

Every evil dream of the past affecting my life now, die, in the name of Jesus.

Every witchcraft serpent attacking me in a dream, die, in the name of Jesus.

Chapter 2 Incubus and Succubus Spirits - Sexual Dreams

When human kind began to multiply on the face of the earth, and daughters were born to them, the sons of God saw that the daughters of humankind were beautiful. Thus they took wives for themselves from any they chose. So the Lord said, "My spirit will not remain in humankind indefinitely, since they are mortal. They will remain for 120 more years."

The Nephilim were on the earth in those days (and also after this) when the sons of God were having sexual relations with the daughters of humankind, who gave birth to their children. Gen. 6:4

The spirit husbands and spirit wives manifest in dreams and in the natural too. These spirits introduce themselves when a person is most vulnerable while they are sleeping. The victims of such hideous acts are targeted because of several reasons, but not limited to this list:

The spirits, which I will refer to as spirit husbands or spirit wives, can be passed down through family generational lines, ancestors who have opened doors and created covenants with these powers.

The spirit husband and spirit wives also gain access from behavior stemming from fornication, molestations, promiscuity, whoredom, homosexuality, lesbianism and masturbation and sexual fantasies. Many people believe fantasizing is innocent. Those who have been raped, sodomized, participated in oral or anal sex are also candidates to the spirit husband or spirit wives. Any practice outside of the marriage bed opens the door through sexual sins. When someone participates in oral or anal sex they are entering into a covenant with demons. The practice of sexual fantasy or imaging yourself sexually with a person is an open door. Evil spirits troubles many who are into pornography. The spirit husband and spirit wives are responsible for causing marital failure and gynecological issues. Why? Because when the door is opened due to pre- marital sex its sin. Many who participated in these activities in sin became one with the person they were involved with. Deliverance is needed to expel evil spirits that were picked up and transferred through these illicit sexual relationships. Many female problems are tied to these spirits. There have been many individuals who could not conceive until they dealt with these spirits through deliverance.

I personally counseled a young woman and she often called because she was dealing with a spirit husband that was having sex with her in the night.
The demon spirits were following her. This person could not get rid of these spirits and was unable to sleep for many nights because she was tormented day and night. This individual decided to sleep with a garbage bag covering her private parts to avoid being sexually abused. Unfortunately, it did not help. She was looking for a natural solution to a spiritual problem. These spirits would even go to church with her. (Yes, I said church). I spoke with her over the phone and she was in Church and told me she could see the demons. I asked her what they were doing? She replied they're right here sniffing me between my legs. They followed her to work and would be sniffing

between her legs. Prayer was not working for her and her problem was growing worse. I often wondered what was going on. These spirits were not obeying to leave her home. When I prayed for her over the phone she would inform me that the demons was listening to our conversation and when I commanded the spirits to leave, according to her, they left her presence and went upstairs to her bedroom.

The demons went up to her bedroom to wait for her to get off the phone. What? I was trying my best to understand why these demons were not obeying the command to leave permanently. I knew something was wrong on her part, but it became clearer as time went on. A couple of weeks after our telephone call, I picked up the phone to call her and a gentleman answered, although during our previous calls I warned her that she should not be fornicating. She quickly stated "Oh no, I'm not have a relationship with anyone." Sometime you take a person at their word because you know they should know better. In fact, she was a minister.

I explained to her the importance of refraining from fornicating closing all doors giving these spirits access and she agreed stating she wasn't fornicating. When the gentleman answered the phone, I knew why she was still being afflicted. I asked her if she was sexually involved again and she answered, "Yes." Now, I know why the demons refuse to leave her alone. She was fornicating all along and they were attached to her because of the sin. Many men and women of the Gospel are actively participating in sexual sins and deal with these types of spirits. The enemy especially likes to afflict those who are in ministry to bring shame to the church. The enemy waits for the right time to expose them (ministers) and bring division and scatter the sheep.

Demonic spirits troubles many people because they refuse to obey the Word of God, turn from sin, renounce, repent, and break soul ties and covenants with the spirit husband or spirit wives. Therefore, these spirits exercise their rights. If you cast them out they come back with additional spirits if the lifestyle does not change.

When the unclean spirit is gone out of a man, he walketh through dry places, seeking rest, and findeth none. Then he saith, I will return into my house from whence I came out; and when he is come, he findeth it empty, swept, and garnished. Then goeth he, and taketh with himself seven other spirits more wicked than himself, and they enter in and dwell there: and the last state of that man is worse than the first. Even so shall it be also unto this wicked generation. Matt 12:43-45

Many people suffer from astral sex, in which satanic agents' project their spirit man into the intended victims' body to have sex. The kingdom of darkness is vile and many satanic agents practice this behavior against each other as well as their unexpected victims.

Prayer point:

Every curse of desolation spoken against my womb, ovary or fallopian tubes by witchcraft; be broken by the blood of Jesus.

(This prayer point is for men) Every power seeking to collect my sperm, fall down and die, in Jesus name.

Any sperm collected from my body, catch fire, in Jesus name.

Many who are violated by incubus or succubus are ashamed to seek help or to reach out to a close friend because of shame. They live as a victim and become a sexual prisoner in their own home.

God is Holy, He is not going to introduce someone to you sexually in your dream as a way of exploring your (sexuality) as some dream interpreter may imply.

As long as someone is in deception the enemy goes unnoticed. God is against fornication, adultery and workers of the flesh. Now the works of the flesh are obvious: sexual immorality, impurity, depravity, idolatry, sorcery, hostilities, strife, jealousy, outbursts of anger, selfish rivalries, dissensions, factions,
envying, murder, drunkenness, carousing, and similar

things. I am warning you, as I had warned you before "[t]hose who practice such things will not inherit the kingdom of God"! Gal 5:19-21 (NIV)

The only one promoting sex in dreams and promoting an opportunity for wet dreams is the devil. I have to come raw because of the perverted information that is being permeated online and in the world. God does not use dreams such as this to get a person to fulfill the works of the flesh. While you are dreaming if there is a man or woman (stranger) lying beside you, it's a spirit husband or spirit wife.

Many people are suffering defeat because of their dream life and because they are unaware of how the enemy is fighting them. The enemy has been waging war through dreams undetected because most people do not know what is taking place.

Prayer points:

Spirit husband/spirit wife; release me by fire, in Jesus name. (Woman say spirit husband and men should say spirit wife) There are cases where the same sex spirit may attack a woman or man. In that case pray the appropriate one or both.

Every spirit husband/ wife, I divorce you by the blood of Jesus.

I break all covenants entered into with the spirit husband or wife, in the name of Jesus.

I command the thunder fire of God to burn to ashes the wedding gown, ring, photographs and all other materials used for the marriage, in Jesus' name.

I send the fire of God to burn to ashes the marriage certificate, in the name of Jesus.

I break every blood and soul-tie covenants with the spirit husband/wife, in the name of Jesus.

I send the thunder fire of God to burn to ashes the children born to the marriage (from the spirit husband/spirit wife), in Jesus' name.

I withdraw my blood, sperm (for men) or any other part of my body deposited on the altar of the spirit husband / wife, in Jesus name.

You spirit husband/spirit wife tormenting my life and earthly marriage, I bind you with hot fetters and chains, in the name of Jesus.

I return to you, every property of yours in my possession in the spirit world, including the dowry and whatsoever was used for the marriage and covenants, in the name of Jesus.

I drain myself of all evil materials deposited in my body as a result of (spirit husband/wife) sexual relations, in Jesus' name.

Lord, send Holy Ghost fire into my private parts and burn out every evil planation deposited by the spirit husband/spirit wife, in the name of Jesus.

I break the head of the snake, deposited into my body by the spirit husband /spirit wife to do me harm, and command it to come out, in the name of Jesus.

I purge out, with the blood of Jesus, every evil material deposited in my womb to prevent me from having children on earth, in the name of Jesus.

Lord, repair and restore all damage done to any part of my body and my earthly marriage by the spirit husband/spirit wife, in the name of Jesus.

I reject and cancel every curse, evil pronouncement, spell, jinx, enchantment and incantation place upon me by the spirit husband/spirit wife, in the name of Jesus.

Chapter 3 Protection Scriptures

Scripture:

Jeremiah 1:19 And they shall fight against thee; but they shall not prevail against thee; for I am with thee, saith the LORD, to deliver thee.

Prayer Point:

All those who fight against me shall not prevail against me, in Jesus name. Amen.

All those who gather together against my children shall fall for my children sake, in Jesus name. Amen.

Scripture:

It is written, "And I will deliver thee out of the hand of the wicked, and I will redeem thee out of the hand of the terrible." Jeremiah 15:21.

Prayer Point:

O lord my God, deliver me out of the hand of the wicked and redeem me out of the hand of the terrible in Jesus name. Amen.

Scripture:

It is written, "The righteous cry and the Lord hears, and deliver them out of all their troubles." Psalm 34:17.

Prayer point:

O God, hear my cry and deliver me from all my troubles, in Jesus name. Amen.

Scripture:

It is written, "No weapon that is formed against thee shall prosper; and every tongue that shall rise against thee in judgment thou shall condemn. This is the heritage of the servants of the Lord, and their righteousness is of me, saith the Lord." Isaiah 54:17.

Prayer Point:

My Father God, I destroy every spiritual or physical weapon formed against me and I condemn every tongue that rises against me in judgment, in Jesus name. Amen.

Scripture:

It is written, "See, I have this day set thee over the nations and over the kingdoms, to root out, and to pull down, to destroy, and to throw down, to build and to plant." Jeremiah 1:10.

Prayer point:

God of Heaven, I root out, I pull down, and I destroy and throw down every power hindering my progress in Jesus' mighty name. Amen.

Scripture:

It is written, "The angel of the Lord encamps round about them that fear him and delivers them." Psalm 34:7.

Prayer point:

Almighty God, send your great angels to encamp round about me, in Jesus name. Amen.

Scripture:

Isaiah 59:19. It is written, "When the enemy shall come in like a flood, the spirit of the Lord shall lift up a standard against him."

Prayer point:
The Lord, Most High, lift up a standard against all the powers of darkness against me, in Jesus name. Amen.

Scriptures for protection
Psalms 27:1- 5

"The Lord is my light and my salvation; Whom shall I fear? The Lord is the strength of my life; Of whom shall I be afraid? When the wicked came against me To eat up my flesh, My enemies and foes, They stumbled and fell. Though an army may encamp against me, My heart shall not fear; Though war may rise against me, In this I will be confident. One thing I have desired of the Lord, That will I seek: That I may dwell in the house of the Lord All the days of my life, To behold the beauty of the Lord, And to inquire in His temple. For in the time of trouble He shall hide me in His pavilion; In the secret place of His tabernacle He shall hide me; He shall set me high upon a rock."

Proverbs 18:10

"The name of the Lord is a strong tower; The righteous run to it and are safe."

Psalms 91:9-10

"Because you have made the Lord, who is my refuge, Even the Most High, your dwelling place, No evil shall befall you, Nor shall any plague come near your dwelling;"

Isaiah 43:1-2

"Fear not, for I have redeemed you; I have called you by your name; You are Mine. When you pass through the waters, I will be with you; And through the rivers, they shall not overflow you. When you walk through the fire, you shall not be burned, Nor shall the flame scorch you."

Ezekiel 34:28

"And they shall no longer be a prey for the nations, nor shall beasts of the land devour them; but they shall dwell safely, and no one shall make them afraid."

Proverbs 1:33

"But whoever listens to me will dwell safely, And will be secure, without fear of evil."

Psalms 121:7-8

"The Lord shall preserve you from all evil; He shall preserve your soul. The Lord shall preserve your going out and your coming in From this time forth, and even forevermore."

Psalms 4:8

"I will both lie down in peace, and sleep; For You alone, O Lord, make me dwell in safety."

Chapter 4 Curses

A curse is an expressed wish to cause misfortune or disaster to befall on one or more persons. The act of execration (cursing) imprecate (invoke or call down) evil or demonic powers upon a person to cause destruction. The consequences of curses are the ability to cause harm, accidents, or death.

The bible tells us "Christ hath redeemed us from the curse of the law, being made a curse for us: for it is written, Cursed is every one that hangeth on a tree: That the blessing of Abraham might come on the Gentiles through Jesus Christ; that we might receive the promise of the Spirit through faith." Galatians 3:13-14

"As the bird by wandering, as the swallow by flying, so the curse causeless shall not come." Proverbs 26:2

If you are a righteous man, a curse without a cause shall not affect you. If you are living in sin, the door is open for a curse to affect you.

Generational curses are also inherited curses from parents, grandparents, or ancestors, who have sinned and opened a doorway for the curses to flow from generation to generation.

There are physical manifestations of curses, the curses of sickness, backwardness, stagnancy, poverty, destruction, unfinished projects, or failure at the edge of your miracle. We must fully under the following scripture with clarity:

"Christ has redeemed us from the curse of the law, being made a curse for us: for it is written, cursed is every one that hanged on a tree: that the blessing of Abraham might come on the Gentiles through Jesus Christ; that we might receive the promise of the spirit through faith. Galatians 3:13-14

Chapter 5 The Unbroken Curses

These curses will continue from generation to generation unless they are broken. When curses are in place blessings are hindered or vanish because of the demonic agents enforcing the curse in ones life.

Some curses are inherited from our father's and mother's house those are generational curses operating before the children are born some of these curses are of poverty, curses of sickness, curses of death at a certain age, curses of backwardness. Open your mouth and say: I break and revoke all curses pronounced by evil people over my life in the Name of Jesus.

Prayer Point:

I renounce every evil incision mark on my body, tongue-piercing resulting in covenants with an evil spirit in the Almighty name of Jesus.

I command all evil spirits in my life associated with any curse or covenant to leave me now in Jesus Name!

By the authority of Jesus My Lord, I break every curse coming from the evil powers of my father's house.

In the Name of Jesus, I destroy every altar that has been erected in my sleep forming any covenants or curses, in Jesus' name.

Every evil dedication in my dream is cancelled by the Blood of Jesus. I paralyze the work of every demonic power, In Jesus' name

I break every curse from the handling of any cursed objects in my dream, in Jesus' name.

Any strange money or cursed gifts received in my dream catch fire, in Jesus name.

I paralyze any contact with demonic agents in my dreams, and any initiations into any witchcraft, in Jesus name.

Every covenant entered into with a spirit husband/ spirit wife in my dream is nullified in the name of Jesus.

I break myself loose from the powers of witches, wizards, spiritual husbands, spiritual wives, spiritual children, spiritual homes, spiritual properties, familiar spirits, water spirits and dead human spirits, in Jesus' name.

I rebuke and bind the demons assigned to the curses in my dreams and neutralize their effects, in Jesus name

I take authority over curses and break every evil covenant and initiations made with me through dreams in the Name of Jesus.

I revoke and break by the Blood of Jesus every evil blood covenant, soul-tie, and evil covenants attached to any satanic agent in my dreams, in Jesus name.

I rebuke and bind the demons assigned to the curses in my dreams and send them to the pit of hell until the day of judgments, in Jesus' Name

Every curse spoken over me in a dream is broken, and reversed into a blessing, in the Mighty Name of Jesus. Amen,

I command all evil spirits associated with any curse broken to leave now, in Jesus name.

Satanic manipulation of my dreams, receive the slap of death in Jesus name.

Power to recollect, retain and translate dark sayings and parables of my dreams elevate my dream life now, in Jesus name.

Every bad dream I have neglected to destroy, I break your backbone and your hold with the hammer of God, in Jesus Name.

Every good dream I had ever received from God since I was born, manifest by fire in Jesus name.

Chapter 6 Breaking Evil Covenants and Curses

Breaking evil covenants and curses is vital to successful living and becoming a friend of God. A covenant is an agreement between two or more persons. The Word of God prohibits any dealings with those who practice abominable customs. We should not incorporate their ways. A person entering into an evil covenant attracts curses and constructs a landing pad for the curses to rest upon them. Covenants are agreements to act in harmony with the one you covenant with. We must break evil covenants and close all demonic doors in our lives. However, when we covenant with God we can experience the abundant life, nothing missing and nothing lacking. James 2:23 And the scripture was fulfilled which saith, Abraham believed God, and it was imputed unto him for righteousness: and he was called the Friend of God. Do you want to be called a friend of God?

Prayer Points:

In the powerful and mighty name of our Lord Jesus Christ, I come against all the spiritual coverings of the powers of darkness in the air, on the land, under the land, in the sea, under the sea, I command every spiritual covering against me to be destroyed.

I destroy every power of darkness that is covering my wealth, health, family, my church, spiritual growth, in the air, on the land, under the land, in the sea, under the sea. I bind all of you hindering demons, in the name of Jesus. I bind you with fetters and chains in the name of Jesus. I send you to the pit of hell until the day of judgment, in the Mighty name of Jesus.

Almighty powerful God in the name of Jesus Christ, Heavenly Father I put on the garment of protection against all the powers of darkness that will attempt to retaliate as they are bombarded by these prayers, I release God's protection over my environment. Holy Ghost fire fall upon and destroy any demon power that is fashioned against me spiritually or physically, as I am praying, in the name of Jesus Christ, Amen.

Any witchcraft tree in my environment, be uprooted, receive the ax of fire; catch fire and burn to ashes, in Jesus name.

Every serpentine power coming against me, catch fire and die, in the name of Jesus. Any evil covenants that I have entered into subconsciously or consciously break, break, break, in Jesus' name.

PRAYER POINTS:

I dissociate myself and my family from every territorial blood covenant, in the name of Jesus.

I dismantle every tribal blood covenant, in the name of Jesus.

I withdraw my blood from every satanic blood bank, in the name of Jesus

Let the blood of any animal shed on my behalf loose its covenant power, (say it three times then you say) loose your covenant power, in the name of Jesus.

Any covenant formed with any organ of my body, be nullified, in the name of Jesus.

I release myself from every curse attached to a blood covenant, in the name of Jesus.

I release myself from every evil collective blood covenant, in the name of Jesus.

(Put your hands on your head and pray this seriously) I release myself from every conscious and unconscious blood covenant, in the name of Jesus.

I break every anti-prosperity covenant, in the name of Jesus.

I break every curse of poverty, in the name of Jesus.

SPIRITUAL WARFARE DURING YOUR SLEEP:
WEAPONS OF WARFARE vol. 2

DR. ALISHA ANDERSON

By Alisha Anderson

Copyright ©2014 by Alisha Anderson

Alisha Anderson

P.O. Box 15716

Durham, NC 27704

www.wmicc.com

Prayer Capsules:

Dr. Alisha Anderson

Table of Content

Chapter 1

What is Dream Warfare?

Spiritual Warfare is conducting combat in the spiritual realm against evil rulers and authorities of the unseen world, against mighty powers in this dark world, and against evil spirits in the heavenly places Eph. 6: 12, many experienced this form of warfare. The Bible says, *(For the weapons of our warfare are not carnal, but mighty through God to the pulling down of strong holds ;) 2 Cor. 10:4.*

Dream warfare also takes place in the spirit realm, but it's during the sleeping hours. It's not during a certain time of the day specifically, but during the time when one is asleep. A person may experience more dream warfare during the night, simply because there is more wicked activity that take place at night.

The best time to deal with dream manipulation is during the night, while demonic agents are releasing incantations (a series of words said as a magic spell, charm, or hexes.) What does one do if they must work during the day, and fight during the night? I recommend that they pray and deal with the powers that have been troubling them during the earlier part of the night (Midnight to 2am). They should start earlier in the night and dismantle every plot programmed against them by practitioner of wickedness. Dream warfare is a different type of warfare, because the person is in a state of rest. During the time of sleeping, a person is more vulnerable. You can take comfort if you have on your spiritual armour while sleeping, knowing you're more

prepared than the average Christian.

Having your feet shod with the preparation of the gospel of peace; above
all, taking the shield of faith, wherewith ye shall be able to quench all the fiery darts of the wicked. And take the helmet of salvation, and the sword of the Spirit, which is the Word of God.

The word level you have in your waking time will come out in your dream state, if needed. By the reading of the Word of God, Praising The Lord, Glorifying God, spending time in prayer, and fasting your will build up your spirit man. A warrior must be full of the Word of God and have an authentic prayer life. How you feed yourself (with the Word) in the natural realm will spill over to the spirit realm. If you are a fiery person in the natural, during your sleeping hours you will be just the same. In other words, a weak Christian will also be weak when experiencing warfare in their dream state. A weak Christian may find he or she is chased away, afraid, and helpless in their dreams. A Christian, who is stronger in the things of God, may find they're using the Word of God to stop their enemies' attacks in their dreams. They will be speaking in their prayer language, calling down fire upon animals sent against them, and causing the weapons of spiritual assassinators to backfire. What does this mean in the natural? It means there are some fights that will already be won in the natural realm, with little or no effort. Instead of suffering losses they will experience increase. Instead of being bound by their enemies, their enemies are left frustrated. When warriors arrive at work they will find that the very people who were opposing them are no longer returning back to the workplace. Those who are overcomers in the spiritual realm will experience greater victories because they have silenced the naysayers, and arrested the troubling powers by the Blood of Jesus. Many do not understand that (a majority of) what they see in their dreams is an indication of what is trying to evolve (develop gradually) in the natural. Dreams are not to be overlooked or downplayed because it appears to be strange or have no significant meaning. You must allow God to tell you whether the dream has been dealt with already, or if it's just a dream of purging, or being consumed with life affairs (Eccl 5:3), or a message that He is conveying to you. (Record your dreams just in case it's a partial message). Do not interpretations belong to God? Don't allow people, who have not sought the Lord concerning your dreams to give vain interpretations or little cute sayings, they have put together to sound extremely prophetic. It is through prayer and seeking God for revelation on the types of prayers that's needed for victory. There is NOTHING HIDDEN from God. Do you remember the story of Elisha when Benhadad King of Syria declared in 2 Kings 6:31 "God do so and more also unto me, if the head of Elisha the son of Shaphat shall stand this day. *2 Kings 6:31-33 He said, "May God deal with me, be it ever so severely, if the head of Elisha son of Shaphat remains on his shoulders today!" Now Elisha was sitting in his house, and the elders were sitting with him. The king sent a messenger ahead, but before he arrived, Elisha said to the elders, "Don't you see how this murderer is sending someone to cut off my head? Look, when the messenger comes, shut the door and hold it shut against him. Is not the sound of his master's footsteps behind him?" While he was still talking to them, the messenger came down to him.*

As the Lord revealed to Elisha the plots of his enemy to cut of his head, God will do the same for you.

No Rules

There are no rules to protect people who choose not to fight back in this type of warfare (Dream Warfare). Most importantly, everyone from time to time can experience dream warfare. Although many have experienced dream warfare, most do not realize the strategies of the enemies against them.

Many do not realize that when they are passive, they're having things stolen, being afflicted, carrying evil loads, receiving infirmities and being victimized in the spirit realm.

Most people know **God Speaks through dreams**, and this is why we should always be prepared to pay attention to our dreams. What good is a warning, if the dreamer does not take heed? God has armed us with weapons for warfare. Our weapons are mighty through God to the pulling down of strongholds. The passive and blasé do not understand the importance of spiritual warfare nor dreams.

Nor, do they desire to ask God for revelation as to "What message is being conveyed?" The Bible tells us "my people are destroyed for lack of knowledge." The enemy has deceived many who say, "Spiritual warfare does not glorify God." All the while the devil is laughing. The truth of the matter is many people are oppressed and held captive by witchcraft chains.

God sent Moses to his people to bring them out of bondage and God is still setting his people free today!!! The

Children of Israel were being oppressed and exploited by hard taskmasters. God sent Moses to personally deliver the message to Pharaoh, God said "Let My People Go."

Pharaoh gave his henchmen instructions to afflict even the more. (gaining your freedom is not always easy- but possible) Pharaoh is a type and shadow of Satan. The taskmasters were instructed by Pharaoh to make it more difficult for the people to perform their tasks of bondage. The people of God were in bitter distress and under great duress that they no longer pursued their freedom. Today, God still desires that His people come out from bondage. After careful observation, some rather stay in their current state of bondage, than to wage war for their deliverance. There is good news!!! Jesus is risen and God will bring restoration to your life, by the same resurrecting power that raise Jesus from the grave. Hallelujah!!!

Covenants
Have respect unto the covenant: for the dark places of the earth are full of the habitations of cruelty. Ps 74:20
One of the areas we need to pay attention to is Covenants

which can be formed conscious or subconsciously. If a person has a demonic covenant existing, the covenants can be used as a door opening to launch a spiritual assault against them. It's vitally important to pray concerning any hidden covenants and address them specifically.

Let me give an example of a covenant that can be formed in the natural realm that will play out in a person's dream. If a person has been participating in masturbation and forms a covenant with the spirit of masturbation, while sleeping they may experience sexual molestation during their sleep. When a person practices this behavior they are covenanting with the spirit of masturbation. (They may also sense a "spirit" getting in their bed performing sexual acts upon them.) I want to make a note, there is a difference in evil spirits attempting to sexually violate someone or a "person" who astral projects to sexually victimize. I will explain more in detail in Chapter 4, **(Astral projection).** Many people have spent countless hours unsuccessfully praying because they have not broken the (evil) covenants that are in place. Covenants are not to be taken lightly nor overlooked. Do you remember the story of Joshua who formed a covenant with the

Gibeonites? Joshua enters into a treaty with the Gibeonites when they came to Joshua with their deceptive plan.

But when the inhabitants of Gibeon heard what Joshua had done to Jericho and Ai, 4 they worked craftily, and went and pretended to be ambassadors. And they took old sacks on their donkeys, old wineskins torn and mended, 5 old and patched sandals on their feet, and old garments on themselves; and all the bread of their provision was dry and moldy. 6 And they went to Joshua, to the camp at Gilgal, and said to him and to the men of Israel, "We have come from a far country; now therefore, make a covenant with us." 7 Then the men of Israel said to the Hivites, "Perhaps you dwell among us; so how can we make a covenant with you?" 8 But they said to Joshua, "We are your servants." And Joshua said to them, "Who are you, and where do you come from?" 9 So they said to him: "From a very far country your servants have come, because of the name of the LORD your God; for we have heard of His fame, and all that He did in Egypt, 10 and all that He did to the two kings of the Amorites who were beyond the Jordan—to Sihon king of Heshbon, and Og king of Bashan, who was at Ashtaroth. 11 Therefore our elders and all the inhabitants of our country spoke to us, saying, 'Take provisions with you for the journey, and go to meet them, and say to them, "We are your servants; now therefore, make a covenant with us."' 12 This bread of ours we took hot for our provision from our houses on the day we departed to come to you. But now look, it is dry and moldy. 13 And these wineskins which we filled were new, and see, they are torn; and these our garments and our sandals have become old because of the very long journey." 14 Then the men of Israel took some of their provisions; but they did not ask counsel of the LORD. 15 So Joshua made peace with them, and made a covenant with them to let them live; and the rulers of the congregation swore to them. 16 And it happened at the end of three days, after they had made a covenant with them, that they heard that they were their neighbors who dwelt near them. 17 Then the children of Israel journeyed and came to their cities on the third day. Now their cities were Gibeon, Chephirah, Beeroth, and Kirjath Jearim. 18 But the children of Israel did not attack them, because the rulers of the congregation had sworn to them by the LORD God of Israel. And all the congregation complained against the rulers.19 Then all the rulers said to all the congregation, "We have sworn to them by the LORD God of Israel; now therefore, we may not touch them.

In the days of Joshua, A covenant was made with the Gibeonites by Joshua (Although the Gibeonites used deception the covenant remained enforced) Israel swore not to harm the Gibeonites, a neighboring tribe (Joshua 9).

God expected Israel to keep their promise, even though the Gibeonites tricked Israel into making the agreement. Saul's killed some of the Gibeonites although there was a covenant in place with the Gibeonites that was made with Joshua.

For whatever is hidden is meant to be disclosed, and whatever is concealed is meant to be brought out into the open. Mark 4:22 There was a famine during David's reign that lasted for three years, so David asked the

LORD about it. And the LORD said, "The famine has come because Saul and his

family are guilty of murdering the Gibeonites." 2 Sam 21:1

David wisely sought God in the face of a persistent problem. This is the same thing you must do. You must seek the Lord as to why specific problems continue to exist. Who wants to find out that they prayed for a situation over the course of years, when all it took was the breaking for a covenant?

He reveals deep and mysterious things and knows what lies hidden in darkness, though he is surrounded by light. Daniel 2:22 So the king summoned the Gibeonites. They were not part of Israel but were all that was left of the nation of the Amorites. The people of Israel had sworn not to kill them, but Saul, in his zeal for Israel and Judah, had tried to wipe them out. 3 David asked them, "What can I do for you? How can I make amends so that you will bless the LORD's people again?" 4 "Well, money can't settle this matter between us and the family of Saul," the Gibeonites replied. "Neither can we demand the life of anyone in Israel." "What can I do then?" David asked. "Just tell me and I will do it for you." 5 Then they replied, "It was Saul who planned to destroy us, to keep us from having any place at all in the territory of Israel. 6 So let seven of Saul's sons be handed over to us, and we will execute them before the LORD at Gibeon, on the mountain of the LORD." 2 Sam 21:2-6

David had to deal with this covenant issue, which caused the famine in the land *first*. Afterward they were able toreap their harvest!!! Covenants must be addressed!!!

"All right," the king (David) said, "I will do it." 7 The king spared Jonathan's son Mephibosheth, who was Saul's grandson, because of the oath David and Jonathan had sworn before the LORD. 8 But he gave them Saul's two sons Armoni and Mephibosheth, whose mother was Rizpah daughter of Aiah. He also gave them the five sons of Saul's daughter Merab, the wife of Adriel son of Barzillai from Meholah. 9 The men of Gibeon executed them on the mountain before the LORD. So all

seven of them died together at the beginning of the barley harvest. 2 Sam 21:7-9

This story shows how they suffered a famine in the land for 3 years because a covenant was broken. This was a covenant, which had to be honoured. If there are covenants of the devil in place, not only should it be BROKEN, but you must also renounce the Sin. Now, if there were unbroken (evil) covenants in place affecting your blessings would you want to know about it? In fact, if you had knowledge of the covenant I'm sure you would not wait to break it. In the process of time, David inquired of the Lord concerning the famine. Is there an area that's lacking in your life? Are you wondering why you have so much resistance in the area of your health, finances, employment, business, education, or marital glory (getting marriage)?

It is possible to enter into a covenant while you are sleeping. **You must remember that satan (your enemy) is a counterfeiter.**

Be sober, be vigilant: because your adversary the devil, as a roaring lion, walketh about, seeking whom he may devour: 1 peter 5:8. The bible tells us that while men slept the enemy came and what did the enemy do? The enemy came and sowed tares among the wheat and went his way…

But while men slept, his enemy came and sowed tares among the wheat and went his way. But when the grain had sprouted and produced a crop, then the tares also appeared. So the servants of the owner came and said to him, 'Sir, did you not sow good seed in your field? How then does it have tares?' He said to them, 'An enemy has done this.' Matthew 13:25-30

Covenant can be established during sleep. *Here is an example of God entering into a covenant with Abram, while Abram was in a deep sleep.*

When Abram was 99 years old, the LORD appeared to Abram and said to him, "I am El Shaddai Walk with me and be trustworthy. 2 I will make a covenant between us and I will give you many, many descendants." 3 Abram fell on his face, and God said to him, 4 "But me, my covenant is with you; you will be the ancestor of many nations. 5 And because I have made you the ancestor of many nations, your name will no longer be Abram but Abraham. 6 I will make you very fertile. I will produce nations from you, and kings will come from you. 7 I will set up my covenant with you and your descendants after you in every generation as an enduring covenant. Gen17:1-7

A Covenant was made between Abram when he was in *a deep sleep*. Let's go back and look at Genesis 15:10-21

10 Abram brought all these to him, cut them in two and arranged the halves opposite each other; the birds, however, he did not cut in half. 11 Then birds of prey came down on the carcasses, but Abram drove them away. {12 As the sun was setting, Abram fell into a deep sleep, and a thick and dreadful darkness came over him.} 13 Then the LORD said to him, "Know for certain that your descendants will be strangers in a country not their own, and they will be enslaved and mistreated four hundred years. 14 But I will punish the nation they serve as slaves, and afterward they will come out with great possessions. 15 You, however, will go to your fathers in peace and be buried at a good old age. 16 In the fourth generation your descendants will come back here, for the sin of the Amorites has not yet reached its full measure." 17 When the sun had set and darkness had fallen, a smoking firepot with a blazing torch appeared and passed between the pieces. 18 On that day the LORD made a covenant with Abram and said, "To your descendants I give this land, from the river of Egypt to the great river, the Euphrates-- 19 the land of the Kenites, Kenizzites, Kadmonites, 20 Hittites, Perizzites, Rephaites, 21 Amorites, Canaanites, Girgashites and Jebusites."

God reminded Isaac and Jacob about the covenant that was spoken to Father Abraham, could God be revealing to you about covenants during your sleep? Are you listening? The point I'm making is covenants can be entered into while a person is asleep. The Word of God tells us, God entered into a covenant with Abram while **Abram was in a deep sleep.** In fact, it was a unilateral covenant, which did not require Abram's involvement. If you have a stubborn case with a persistent problem, look (spiritually) to see if you're dealing with an unbroken (demonic) covenant. An example of a covenant still in place can be seen when someone has sexual relations outside of marriage. When they are no longer together, they may think of each other at the same time. When one thinks of the other person the phone (suddenly) rings and he or she is on the other line. When it appears they can't function without each another it displays a fragmented soul, desperately in need of healings. It's not only a soul-tie involved but a covenant is in place too.

DEAL WITH THE COVENANTS IN PLACE.

The Bible is our blue print.

Marriage is a covenant, two people coming together as "one" is a covenant. Therefore shall a man leave his father and his mother,
and shall cleave unto his wife: and they shall be one flesh. (Genesis 2:24, KJV). For this reason a man will leave his father and mother and be united to his wife, and they will become one flesh. (Genesis 2:24, NIV).

Therefore a man leaves his father and his mother and clings to his wife, and they become one flesh. (Genesis 2:24, NRSV).

Those who do not break the soul ties will find themselves still connected spiritually. An invisible line is still attached to them wherever they go, because they are one. When either one of them gets married, the invisible line climbs into the bed with them too. It is imperative that we cancel demonic dream attacks and break any covenants that we may have formed in our sleep. In order to experience liberty and restoration we must be transparent with ourselves. David prayed that he would not deceive himself, we should we should do likewise.

Chapter 3

Breaking Evil Covenants

Confessions: col. 2:14-15: Blotting out the handwriting of ordinances that was against us, which was contrary to us, and took it out of the way, nailing it to his cross; And having spoiled principalities and powers, he made a shew of them openly, triumphing over them in it. Galatians 3:13-14: Christ hath redeemed us from the curse of the law, being made a curse for us: for it is written, cursed is everyone that hangeth on a tree: That

the blessing of Abraham might come on the Gentiles through Jesus Christ; that we might receive the promise of the Spirit through faith.

There are further steps that must be taken when breaking evil covenants. Once you have broken the covenants in place, deal with the demons attached to those covenants.

Ask the Lord where you should send them (demons), or send them to the pit of hell until the day of judgment, in Jesus name. Below are some sample prayers for breaking soul ties and evil covenants. You should ask the Holy Spirit to lead you and pray them several times before moving on to the next

prayer capsule. I recommend that you do not skip over the prayers just because you think it does not apply to you. No prayer is ever wasted. In fact some covenants could possibly be hidden or entered into unconsciously. Also, some covenants may require more aggressive prayers.

1) Every Soul tie and covenant between me and the spirit of fornication break, in Jesus name.

2) Every Soul tie and covenant between me and the spirit of perversion break, in Jesus name.

3) Every Soul tie and covenant between me and witchcraft break, in Jesus name

4) Every Soul tie and covenant between me and (place ex-boyfriends/ girlfriends/ ex-husbands name here) break, in Jesus name.

5) Every Soul tie and Covenant between me and _____, break, in the mighty name of Jesus.

***Now allow the HOLY SPIRIT to lead you as to any other covenants that need to be broken…

Remember to ask God to reveal the secret hidden things you must deal with. Once you receive revelation of any additional covenants to be broken you can follow the steps above. Maybe you do not have a covenant in place with fornication, but what about:

Divorces in your family

Covenants with personal destructive behavior

Covenants with suicide (some people have multiple suicide attempts in their family line)

Covenants/curses with sicknesses/infirmities

REMEMBER: The covenant that caused the famine noted in 2 Sam 21 was entered into by Joshua and the Gibeonites but the famine and covenant effected another generation, which had to addressed by King David.

6 Seek ye the LORD while he may be found, call ye upon him while he is near: 7 Let the wicked forsake his way, and the unrighteous man his thoughts: and let him return unto the LORD, and

he will have mercy upon him; and to our God, for he will abundantly pardon. Is 55:6-7

Strange Dreams may not be so strange after all. I've mentioned several times that covenants can be formed during the sleep process. Also, know that some people are initiated into witchcraft in their sleep? How can you tell?

If a person is attending witchcraft meetings, cooking in witchcraft pots, walking in the river or in the ocean they may have been initiated into secret demonic societies in their sleep. (The marine kingdom operates from the waters). Now, please don't be so fast to rule out certain dreams. Many people do not recall their dreams or they remember just bits and pieces that appeared to be strange. The normal tendency is to ignore the dream. After reading this book I pray you don't ignore your dreams again. I do not want you to get offended, but the notion that what you don't know can't hurt you will never work here. The more you pray serious warfare prayers or prayer points challenging evil powers, ask God to reveal to you what you are fighting against. Once God speaks to you and reveals the powers behind your problem, you can now hit the specific target with perfection. Bulls-Eyes!!! I've asked God to reveal the secrets behind my problems and I must admit that I was astonished at what was revealed. Abram covenanted while he was asleep, which was a unilateral covenant. Covenants can effect future generations if left intact as pointed out above.

Identifying Warfare Dreams

Eating in dreams may appear quite harmless but these types of dreams are the strategies of dream invaders.

Note: There are dreams in which the Lord may prepare a banquet for you in the presence of your enemy or God may speak specifically to you using food symbolically. Remember satan is a counterfeiter and use food as a weapon to pollute and manipulate lives. (More so, the enemy is attempting to pollute, poison, or plant evil plantations.)

There are plenty of case studies in which people are afflicted and remembered they ate food in their dreams. Many women have been given certain foods in their sleep and miscarried. Those who attempt to manipulate people during their sleep love to use "witchcraft feedings". It's just the same in the natural, they love feeding their potential victims with food and giving candy (hint…hint). These types of dreams should not only be well noted but upon waking from a dream of eating ask God to uproot anything that's not of Him. It's important not to rush the process and vomit up any evil plantations. Dreams where one is eating can plant sickness, lukewarmness (loss of interest in the things of God), miscarriages and initiations into witchcraft; it should not be taken likely. We should be on the offensive vs. the defensive. Upon waking make sure you erase any evil marks placed on you in the spirit. There are many people who are conducting rituals, go to witchcraft meeting, and bowing down to evil altars in their sleep (some may hold positions of a high priest in the astral world in their dreams).

These types of dreams definitely should not be written off. Dreams such as these indicate idols worship, family shines, and evil sacrifices. (If you think it pertains to only Africa, think again) It is also possible for someone to have a position in the kingdom of darkness and not realize they are ministering under a demonic anointing in the natural. This is what the devil wants and he will use any open door to pollute the lives of people. Why should the children of God who have been afflicted not be taught how to come out of witchcraft, receive their deliverance and walk in the freedom of Jesus Christ? Maybe you are not familiar with people who are in bondage due to witchcraft but why should they not be FREE!!! If many of us will be honest, we ourselves experienced bondages too.

BONDAGE IS NOT FUN, IT TORMENTS. Anyone who does deliverance should know that it is by the Power of God that people are set free. Everyone should seek to undergo a deeper deliverance session, which deals with placenta manipulations, foundational problems, and ancestral powers, etc. There are many people who need help but they do not have anyone to go to because people will just tell them a to believe God or say a short prayer, but there is further ministry that's needed. I thank Jesus The Son of God who showed us first hand that He came to liberate the captives.

The Spirit of the Sovereign Lord is upon me, for the Lord has anointed me to bring good news to the poor. He has sent me to comfort the brokenhearted and to proclaim that captives will be released and prisoners will be freed. He has sent me to tell those who mourn that the time of the Lord's favor has come, and with it, the day of God's anger against their enemies. To all who mourn in Israel, he will give a crown of beauty for ashes, a joyous blessing instead of mourning, festive praise instead of despair. In their righteousness, they will be like great oaks that the Lord has planted for his own glory. Is 61:1-3

Many people travel to other states and countries for deeper deliverance sessions because many Churches do not conduct deliverance sessions. Who is willing to help those who need deeper deliverance? It's not about giving the devil the Glory because satan hates the Remnant, and those who are sent to help set the captives free. Witchcraft practices are allowed in many Churches (witches and wizards are allow to minister to God's people). There are countless stories about how the enemy has closed churches, caused division and made some ministries powerless with man pleasing words, etc. Many demonic agents are working in the Churches today (full-time). The assignments of demonic agents are to cause destruction, make the Church services powerless and the scatter the sheep. It is under the direction of God, and not man's opinion that we as ministers must do what we were called to do. I can do nothing of myself, but what I'm instructed of The Father to do.

Then answered Jesus and said unto them, Verily, verily, I say unto you, The Son can do nothing of himself, but what he seeth the Father do: for what things soever he doeth, these also doeth the Son likewise. John 5:19

Everyone needs deliverance "No exception". Deliverance ministers should be studying the Word of God, worshipping, Praying, Fasting, Praising God, and surrendered to the will of God. If a person is moving by

the Spirit of God, they can only do, say, preach or teach the message that God has given to them; pray and ask God about what you may not understand. It's important not to fight against God's work just because we don't have revelation (now) as to what He is doing through his ministers.

38 "So my advice is, leave these men alone. Let them go. If they are planning and doing these things merely on their own, it will soon be overthrown. 39 But if it is from God, you will not be able to overthrow them. You may even find yourselves fighting against God!" Act 5: 38-39

When captives are set free, God Gets the Glory!!! Yes, God does get the Glory!!! The people rejoice, they Glorify and Praise God for visiting their situations, delivering them from suicide, perversions, destroying strongholds etc. They (captives) praise The Lord for his compassion to set the captive free. Most people have family and friends who may be considered as being collective captives. They are the ones who will tell you "it does not take all of that praying" or question if "you actually believe that stuff" or scornfully

echo, "Everything with you is Jesus, Jesus, Jesus". These are the same individuals who believe that God will take care of them although they do not do anything but sit and wait on the Lord. These are the collective captives who believe solely in fate and lament that they cannot change anything. Sadly, these are the same people who do not believe God exists and can move mountains.

In other words, collective captives are "oblivious" that they are prisoners. They live in denial and choose to do nothing because they are content with "life" as they call it. They are unable to comprehend because they are carnal. However, if you have family members or friends who have been taken captive by the enemy, there is hope. Isaiah 49:24-26 asks the question "[c]an spoils be taken from a warrior, or captives be rescued from a conqueror?"

"Indeed," says the Lord, "captives will be taken from a warrior; spoils will be rescued from a conqueror. I will oppose your adversary and I will rescue your children."

This is good news for us because our God will fight for us; we have liberty and victory in Christ Jesus!

"The spirit of the sovereign Lord is upon me because the Lord has chosen me. *He has commissioned me to encourage the*

poor, to help the brokenhearted to decree the release of captives, and the freeing of prisoners." (Is 61:1.)

We must remember that this war is spiritual. It cannot be seen in the natural until it comes into manifestation. The battle is won or lost before you see it manifested in the physical. Many Christians suffer defeat wondering why

life has turned out a certain way for them, and this is why I have written this book! One of the purposes of this book is to raise your awareness about attacks directed against you in your dreams. Dreaming is an area we do not seemingly have authority over. This is why many people are eager to have the interpretation of their dreams. They want to be able to 'foresee' what will happen in 'their future' or perhaps understand the meaning of the dream. If the dreams are positive, they are happy, but when their dreams are negative they become fearful. We cannot continue to do absolutely nothing concerning our dreams. Yes, I said nothing. Having the interpretation of your dream solely is nothing. (If you have a prophetic dream you have to do something!!!) Are you covering your prophetic dreams with the Blood of Jesus? **Anyway, you need Wisdom concerning what to do pertaining to any interpretation and the ability to implement**. I must make this point clear before moving on: *Then Joseph said to Pharaoh, "The dreams of Pharaoh are one; God has revealed to Pharaoh what he is about to do. 26 The seven good cows are seven years, and the seven good ears are seven years; the dreams are one. 27 The seven lean and ugly cows that came up after them are seven years, and the seven empty ears blighted by the east wind are also seven years of famine. 28 It is as I told Pharaoh; God has shown to Pharaoh what he is about to do. 29 There will come seven years of great plenty throughout all the land of Egypt, 30 but after them there will arise seven years of famine, and all the plenty* *will be forgotten in the land of Egypt. The famine will consume the land, 31 and the plenty will be unknown in the land by reason of the famine that will follow, for it will be very severe. 32 And the doubling of Pharaoh's dream means that the thing is fixed by God, and God will shortly bring it about. 33 Now therefore let Pharaoh select a discerning and wise man, and set him over the land of Egypt. 34 Let Pharaoh proceed to appoint overseers over the land and take one-fifth of the produce of the land of Egypt during the seven plentiful years. 35 And let them gather all the food of these good years that are coming and store up grain under the authority of Pharaoh for food in the cities, and let them keep it. 36 That food shall be a reserve for the land against the seven years of famine that are to occur in the land of Egypt, so that the land may not perish through the famine."* 37 This proposal pleased Pharaoh and all his servants. 38 And Pharaoh said to his servants, **"Can we find a man like this, in whom is the Spirit of God?" 39 Then Pharaoh said to Joseph, "Since God has shown you all this, there is none so discerning and wise as you are. 40 You shall be over my house, and all my people**

shall order themselves as you command. Only as regards the throne will I be greater than you." Gen 41:25-40 Joseph gave the interpretation through God, then it was implemented and put into action. Glory to God!!! Cancel destructive dreams.

A large percentage of people fail to cancel their dreams *properly*, and make statements such as "the devil is a liar". Well, we know the devil is a liar why waste time on the obvious. The first crucial step is to cancel the dreams specifically. We must understand that unchallenged negative dreams will only produce a negative harvest. We must not just say general prayers or praying amiss, wasting bullets (Prayer) by hitting the wrong targets. We need to put on our spiritual armor and send air strikes against the powers afflicting us in our sleep.

Chapter 4
Astral Projection
Astral projection (or **astral travel**) is an out-of-body experience practice, which is demonic in its entirety. Astral projection is not to be mistaken with the Lord

allowing someone to be caught up taking them to see something in the spirit realm. (*I was caught up to the third heaven fourteen years ago. Whether I was in my body or out of my body, I don't know—only God knows.) 2 Cor 12:2-4*

Here is another account:

11 Moreover the spirit lifted me up, and brought me unto the east gate of the LORD's house, which looketh eastward: and behold at the door of the gate five and twenty men; among whom I saw Jaazaniah the son of Azur, and Pelatiah the son of Benaiah, princes of the people. 2 Then said he unto me, Son of man, these are the men that devise mischief, and give wicked counsel in this city:

Ezekiel 11:1-2

And he put forth the form of a hand, and took me by a lock of mine head; and the spirit lifted me up between the earth and the heaven, and brought me in the visions of God to Jerusalem, to the door of the inner gate that looketh toward the north; where was the seat of the image of jealousy, which provoketh to jealousy. 4 And, behold, the glory of the God of Israel was there, according to the vision that I saw in the plain. 5 Then said he unto me, Son of man, lift up thine eyes now the way toward the north. So I lifted up mine eyes the way toward the north, and behold northward at the

gate of the altar this image of jealousy in the entry. 6 He said furthermore unto me, Son of man, seest thou what they do? even the great abominations that the house of Israel committeth here, that I should go far off from my sanctuary? but turn thee yet again, and thou shalt see greater abominations. 7 And he brought me to the door of the court; and when I looked, behold a hole in the wall. 8 Then said he unto me, Son of man, dig now in the wall: and when I had digged in the wall, behold a door. 9 And he said unto me, Go in, and behold the wicked abominations that they do here. 10 So I went in and saw; and behold every form of creeping things, and abominable beasts, and all the idols of the house of Israel, portrayed upon the wall round about. Ezekiel 8:3-9

Any out of body experience outside of the Lord is witchcraft and forbidden. Those who use astral projection are being guided by demons. Many people have experience seeing or sensing someone astral projecting into their homes. Now for those who practice astral projection, understand that it's very dangerous *for you* and **wicked**. I previously gave an example in (Spiritual Warfare During Your Sleep vol.1) of a young woman who stated that her mother ask her to check on her from time to time to see if she was still breathing; while she covered her face with a handkerchief lying in the bed. Her mother was a witch and was astral projecting during a demonic assignment. The daughter was wondering why their household was being bombarded with spiritual attacks.

Actually, *many people know the answer to their dilemma*; her mother and the other witches were fighting among themselves to gain more satanic power and demonic positions. It is important to make sure you are protected. I cannot stress the importance. Again, if you are conducting spiritual warfare you should pray prayers of protections over yourself and your family before going to sleep. You need to make sure you cover yourself after speaking with people on the phone, prior to lying down. Demons can travel through phone lines. After speaking or ministering over the phone bind any evil transference.

There are times in which someone may get a glimpse of something that quickly. Have you ever thought you seen something move in your peripheral vision? Perhaps, you've seen dark moving objects or shadows vertically alongside the wall; these are the works of demonic forces.

Many times God will open your eyes to see demonic activities in your environment or coming against your home. Maybe you think you are seeing something crawling, flying, or moving around you, (and realize it's nothing there- you're seeing it in the spirit) immediately start praying. This is an indication something is going on in the spirit realm, you should also close any door open to the enemy. If you have been arguing or opened a breach in the spirit, close those doors. GET IT RIGHT WITH EVERYONE IN THE HOME, you should all be on one accord. One man can put 1,000 to flight and two men can put 10000 to flight, with the Lord on your side. Also, if you start to see an increase of insects, cats, roaches, lizards, spiders etc. A person may be under satanic monitoring and should command the fire of God to consume all evil eyes and monitoring devises. When you command the fire of God to burn these demonic monitoring agents astral projection through these critters, they will disappear. If you experienced the hair on your arms standing up, strange sensations; begin to pray and cover yourself with the blood of Jesus.

In the Book of Job, he states *15 Then a spirit passed before my face; the hair of my flesh stood up: Job 4:5*

Your *first reaction* may be to second guess yourself and think it was nothing at all. In Chapter 2, I've discussed covenants but I want to give an example of sexual attacks some have suffered by demonic agents astral projecting and/ or demons during their sleep. Perhaps, you don't know anyone who has
experience this, your maybe you haven't either, but plenty of people have come under attack and they're not sleeping

because of fear because of these attacks. When I was about 12 years old, one of my childhood friends told me of about a spiritual problem she was having being sexually attacked by demons. At the time I didn't know what to tell her. This was the first time I've heard of such a thing. Why would she tell me instead of an adult? I was always going to church and maybe she felt I would not say she was crazy. All I knew to do was take her to the Pastor for help. In this day and time, I hear of similar situations quite often. In almost all cases the people have open the door through sexual promiscuity. (Some attacked are by the succubus and incubus spirits; and passed down the family line. Therefore, not EVERYONE has opened a door personally). The childhood friend told me about shortly after her dilemma that she was having sexual relations with different men.

Most people have lascivious (immoral sexual *thoughts* or actions) which also open the door to attacks while asleep If a person has been participating in masturbation and formed a covenant with the spirit of masturbation, while sleeping they may experience (demonic) spirits molesting them.

They may also sense a "being" getting in their bed performing sexual acts upon them. I want to note that there is a difference between evil spirits attempting to violate someone and a person who astral projects to molest. If you experienced these types of activities in your home it's time to draw out your weapons. You must bind the demon powers with fetters and chains, in Jesus Name. You should command the silver cord of anyone astral projecting into your home to detach and catch fire, in Jesus name. Also, set ley line on fire and command all witchcraft vehicles to explode, in Jesus name. There are satanic agents who may desire to have intercourse with someone and they plan to astral project to their potential victim's home. This attack is different in that it's a human doing this (through Astral Projection) so you will deal with this differently than demonic spirits. Nevertheless, if you cannot discern which one you are dealing with, pray as previous instructed and pray against both. You must seek God in all things, because spiritual manipulators can also use someone else's image attempting to throw you off. (I call this "fighting shadows") You *can* call on the name of Jesus and by His authority arrest these powers.

In the book of Ecclesiastes *12:6-7 it speaks of the silver cord: 6 Or ever the silver cord be loosed, or the golden bowl be broken, or the pitcher be broken at the fountain, or the wheel broken at the cistern. 7 Then shall the dust return to the earth as it was: and the spirit shall return unto God who gave it.*

9 Wherefore God also hath highly exalted him, and given him a name which is above every name: 10 That at the name of Jesus every knee should bow, of things in heaven, and things in earth, and things under the earth; (Phil. 2:9-10)

If you are experiencing frequent episodes in which you a seeing this type of activities in your home, you need to deal with monitoring powers, astral projection, open doors and demons sent against you. (This is not the time to show mercy.) Make sure you command fire upon the silver cord or severed the silver cord.

Before the silver cord is severed, and the golden bow is broken; before the pitcher is shattered at the spring, and the wheel broken at the well Ecclesiastes 12:6 You should command anything representing you in the astral world to catch fire. (Pictures, hair, nails, clothing etc.) Wherefore God also hath highly exalted him, and given him a name which is above every name:

That at the name of Jesus every knee should bow, of things in heaven, and things in earth, and things under the earth; (Phil. 2:9-10) The Television and mirrors can also serve as a gateway by the enemy for astral projection. By the Spirit of God, during a TV commercial I was able to see (in the spirit) a

witch throw some particles of dust (towards the camera), which gives the appearance of throwing it at the viewer and I saw the dust fall on my floor and a figure like (genie) jump out the TV. I immediately arrested those powers, in Jesus name and came against astral projection, incantations, enchantments, etc. in Jesus Name. My preference is to have the TV off. Have you noticed all the demonic commercials now? A person would practically have to hold the remote in their hands and turn off the TV just to walk into the kitchen. If a person is having a dream and see mirrors in their dreams they should command evil mirrors to break to irreparable pieces upon waking, in Jesus name.

Demonic people also use mirrors to summons people or use the person's image (Photos, etc.) to bring the person to them. What do I mean to bring the person to them?

Read the Biblical story of Saul going to the witch of Endor 1 Sam 28:7-13 (7 **Saul then said to his attendants, "Find me a woman who is a medium, so I may go and inquire of her." "There is one in Endor," they said.** 8 So Saul disguised himself, putting on other clothes and at night he and two men went to the woman. "Consult a spirit for me," he said, "and bring up for me the one I name." 9 But the woman said to him, "Surely you know what Saul has done. He has cut off the mediums and spiritists from the land. Why have you set a trap for my life to bring about my death?" 10 Saul swore to her by the LORD, "As surely as the LORD lives, you will not be punished for this."

11 **Then the woman asked, "Whom shall I bring up for you?" "Bring up Samuel," he said.** 12 When the woman

saw Samuel, she cried out at the top of her voice and said to Saul, "Why have you deceived me? You are Saul!"

13 The king said to her, "Don't be afraid. What do you see?" The woman said, "**I see a spirit coming up out of the ground.") This act was forbidden and King Saul tapped into the demonic realm out of desperation.**

The person who is sleeping may see himself or herself in a mirror while dreaming or perhaps the Lord is revealing demonic manipulate using your images. If so, make sure you pray to neutralize and paralyze all satanic manipulations using your images. You should also cover your photos and items with the Blood of Jesus. You can command them to catch fire in the Astral World or in the marine kingdom, wherever they may be. Don't be intimated!!! JESUS HAS ALL POWER AND YOU CAN CALL ON JESUS OR THINK "JESUS" TO OVERCOME your enemies while sleeping unable to speak or move. **There is power in the Name of Jesus.** *The chief priests and the Pharisees sent soldiers and guards with Judas. They had lamps, and torches, and things to fight with. Jesus knew everything that was going to happen to* *him. So he went out and said to them, who are you looking for? They answered, `Jesus from Nazareth.'*

Jesus said to them, `I am he.' Judas, who had given Jesus over to them, was standing with them. When Jesus said to them, `I am he,' they all drew back suddenly and fell down. (Every knee must bow and every tongue must confess that Jesus is Lord!!!) 7 So Jesus asked them again, `Who are you looking for?' And they said, `Jesus from Nazareth.' 8 Then Jesus answered, `I have already told you that I am he. If you are looking for me, let these men go.' (**JESUS WILL NEVER LEAVE OR FORSAKE THOSE WHO BELONG TO HIM!!!** You can fight back with the Blood of Jesus. *Revelation 12:11 "And they overcame him (Satan) by the blood of the Lamb, and by the word of their testimony ..."*

Remember!!! When you see them, feel any vibrations in your proximity; sense an ungodly presence close to you CUT AND BURN THE SILVER CORD, IN THE NAME OF JESUS.

Ephesian 6:11-13 *Put on the full armor of God, so that you will be able to stand firm against the schemes of the devil. For our struggle is not against flesh and blood, but against the rulers, against the powers, against the world forces of this darkness, against the spiritual forces of wickedness*

in the heavenly places. Therefore, take up the full armor of God, so that you will be able to resist in the evil day, and having done everything, to stand firm. I have to interject and mention that these scriptures are in the Bible for a purpose, God would not leave us ignorant of the devil devices.

Summoning one to fly.

There is scriptural text that speaks to summoning one to fly. Here is another practice commonly done by those who practice witchcraft:

"Therefore thus saith the Lord GOD; behold, I am against your pillows, wherewith ye there hunt the souls to make them fly, and I will tear them from your arms, and will let the souls go, even the souls that ye hunt to make them fly." Ezek 13:20

While some are sleeping they have felt themselves being summons. I know of someone who was sleeping when demonic agents were trying to bring her to their witchcraft meetings (coven). The plot of the enemy was to summons her to a witchcraft coven to deal with her because of her ministry work. It was the saving grace of God and His protection that the enemy's plan was foiled. She realized that she needed to pray more fiery prayers for protection.

If you are conducting spiritual warfare you should pray prayers of protection over yourself, your family, and possession before going to sleep. You must pray prayers that will paralyze the operations of the enemy to stop your enemies in their tracks, and render them impotent (unable to take effective action; helpless or powerless.). I'm reminded of a short time ago when the ministry received a phone call. A young woman stated that her mother would ask her to check on her from time to time to see if she was still breathing, while she covered her face with a handkerchief lying in the bed. Her mother was a witch who was allowing her spirit to travel on demonic assignments. Her daughter was wondering why their household was being bombarded with spiritual attacks.

Actually, many people know the answer to their dilemma; her mother and the other witch were fighting among themselves to gain more power. Many people ask for prayers on their behalf, but they are still actively involved with the occult. This person (her mother) was astral projecting her spirit for witchcraft purposes. It is important to make sure you are protected. I cannot

stress the importance enough. Again, if you are conducting spiritual warfare you should pray prayers of protections over yourself and your family before going to sleep. You need to make sure you cover yourself with the Blood of Jesus after speaking with people on the phone, prior to lying down. Prayers that will paralyze the enemies operations, to backfire every arrow sent your way. *It is also important to paralyze and neutralize any elements the enemy may try to use against you. – Earth, wind, fire, or water, in Jesus name.*

No weapon that is formed against us shall prosper and every tongue, which rises against us in judgment, we do condemn. This is our heritage as servants of the Lord and our righteousness is from You, O Lord of Hosts. Is 54:17

In righteousness shalt thou be established: thou shalt be far from oppression; for thou shalt not fear: and from terror; for it shall not come near thee. Behold, they shall surely gather together, but not by me: whosoever shall gather together against thee shall fall for thy sake. Is 54:14-15

Dreaming is definitely one of the ways God speaks to us, providing us with information, directions, and warnings. The dreams we dream also show what is taking place, or plots of the enemy (what you need to pray against) in the spiritual realm. If do not take your dreams seriously or do not remember your dreams, an evil exchange could be taking place. An example of an evil exchange is when you are spending money in the spirit realm or giving away your money, or trading your wealth for poverty. It is when something good is being stolen and replaced with something evil. It's time to pursue, overtake, and recover all!!!

Ley Lines

If someone or something materializes in your home and you see it from your peripheral as a flash, cut the silver cord, in the name of Jesus. Remember, you have spiritual weapons. Just say this, in the name of Jesus Christ of Nazareth, I take the sword of the spirit and I cut and burn all ungodly silver cords and ley lines. Ley Line is travel routes that witches or warlock use to travel in the astral world. These lines can exist though businesses, homes, communities etc.

The purpose of mentioning about ley line is so you will not have travel routes through your home or leading up to your home. If this sounds strange to you, pray and ask The Lord to give you more understanding in regards to this. (It's ok, to place something you don't quite understand on the shelf until God gives more understand or revelation about the matter as you are seeking Him.) I still have to mention it because there are some who will receive confirmation to their prayer petitions asking God to speak to them about some of their dream warfare matters. There are others that have already experienced or know someone who experienced the situations I'm describing.

This book is not a book to take anyone one a witch-hunt, but to impart knowledge that's much needed. Many people don't know who to turn to for help and God does not want us INGORANT of the devil's devices.

Your Bethel

When you move to a new location, before taking occupancy…Pray more than general prayers and do some serious house cleaning prayer. CAST DOWN (evil altars and demonic thrones) that may have been establish there by other tenants. There is no reason you should carry anyone else's evil loads or the problems of the previous occupants. Your dwelling place should a place of peace. You must take authority over the territorial powers where you live.

Your dreams can reveal what is taking place in your neighborhood, community, city or region. Some people have loss possessions, suffered many difficulties because of where they live and not dealing with strongholds over their city. This book will not address Territorial powers, but I want to mention that you should only seek God and be led. There are some battles you must prepare for and have your Fighting Orders and detailed strategies from the Lord. (The Lord may want you to only deal with Territorial Powers as it pertains to taking authority over your home. IN OTHER WORDS, MORE TRAINING IS REQUIRED FOR SOME BATTLES. Then Moses said to him, "If you don't go with us, don't send us up from here. EX. 35:15

NOW LETS GET BACK TO YOUR BETHEL…When Jacob came to a resting place, he spent the night there and had a dream. The heavens were opened to him, and Jacob saw angelic activities. Jacob experienced a visitation from God. He (Jacob) did not know it but he pitches his tent at the house of God- Bethel-means House of God (A holy place). **The place were Jacob rested was at a location where an altar was previously raised unto the Lord!!!** Many years earlier his grandfather **Abraham** had **built an altar to the Lord there. Locations does Matter!!!**

He came to a certain place and spent the night there, because the sun had set; and he took one of the stones of the place and put it under his head, and lay down in that place. He had a dream, and behold, a ladder was set on the earth with its top reaching to heaven; and behold, the angels of God were ascending and descending on it. And behold, the LORD stood above it and said, "I am the LORD, the God of your father Abraham and the God of Isaac; the land on which you lie, I will give it to you and to your descendants...Gen 28:11-14 16 **Then Jacob awoke from his sleep and said, "Surely the LORD is in this place, and I wasn't even aware of it!"** 17 *But he was also afraid and said, "What an awesome place this is! It is none other than the house of God, the very* **gateway to heaven!" Gen 28:16- 17**

Pray over your dwelling place, and dedicate your home/apt to the lord before taking occupancy.

Chapter 5

Spiritual Caging

...'For wicked men are found among My people, They watch like fowlers lying in wait; They set a trap, They

catch men. 'Like a cage full of birds, so their houses are full of deceit; therefore they have become great and rich. Jer 5:26-27

What is spiritual caging? Many people who have been caged in one form or another remember some dream of being tied with ropes, locked in a house, cage, or room. This form of entrapment in a dream shows there's a restriction upon the person's life or the enemy is plotting to cage them in the spirit realm. In the natural cages are to contain items, animals and people. In the penal system many men and women are caged in the natural, but some people can be caged spiritually too. A person can have their health caged, marriage, finances, degrees, etc. I have knowledge of a company where witchcraft manipulation is a common practice. There were about 15 or more of these agents who would use various tactics attempting to trap and enslave their unsuspecting victims. One day, one of these agents was trying to cage a person by placing a satanic box on the connecting cubicle. They would move the box around the entire cubicles trying to set traps. Here is what the word of God says about those who practice these abominable acts:

Your iniquities have turned away these things, and your sins have withholden good things from you. For among my people are found wicked men: they lay wait, as he that setteth snares; they set a trap, they catch men.

There are some who dreamed they were locked in a building and could not get out. The enemy is trying to cage a person when they see themselves locked up in prison, handcuffed, in a pit, etc. (in a dream). This is just one of the many wicked devices of witchcraft manipulators. Sometimes you may not know the full interpretation of the dream but the part you do know, you can foil the diabolical assignments sent against you. When a person is held captive in a cage it's like an invisible string keeping them within a certain boundary. They experience limitation in various areas of their life regardless of their educational level. Spiritual cages must be broken or dismantled because moving from location to location or changing job etc., the captive will still be caged.

26 For among my people are found wicked men: they lay wait, as he that setteth snares; they set a trap, they catch men. 27 As a cage is full of birds, so are their houses full of deceit: therefore they are become great, and waxen rich. 28 They are waxen fat, they shine: yea, they overpass the deeds of the wicked: they judge not the cause, the cause of the fatherless, yet they prosper; and the right of the needy do they not judge. 29 Shall I not visit for these things? saith the LORD: shall not my soul be avenged on such a nation as this? 30 A wonderful and horrible thing is committed in the land; 31 The prophets prophesy falsely, and the priests bear rule by their means; and my people love to have it so: and what will ye do in the end thereof? Jer 5:25-31

After careful study of this passage, it reveals that false prophets prophesy and can cage the lives of people too. The scripture point to God's people desiring the false words. I've heard many stories on how false prophets have spoken words and laid hands on the people of God for impartation. Many people are held captive to the demonic words spoken over them. This is also a form of caging too. Although the spiritual cage cannot be seen with the natural eyes, there are different types of cages.

What comes to me is the invisible fence that was created to allow dogs or animals to move around within the confines of the owner's property. The animals with the invisible fence may have more freedom than the animals in small cages but A cage is a cage. It doesn't matter if it is a 5x5, 5x10, 5x25, or a yard. The person is impeded from experiencing total freedom. These types of cages, fence, and gates can be deceptive in that it appears to all that the animal can come and go, past the owners' property. Once the animal breaches the boundaries they may hear and audible tone connected to a computerized collar which programs them to stay inbound. Upon further programming the animal will be conditioned to go no further than the boundaries unless instructed to do so. Many are under this same type of bondage by false words released over their lives. This form of caging prevents them from walking out the Call of God upon their lives. You must be determine today to break every spiritual cage in Jesus name.

Prayer Capsule:

I arrest every spiritual attacker and paralyze their activities in my life, in the name of Jesus.

O Lord, perform the necessary surgical operation in my life and change all that has gone wrong in the spirit world, in Jesus' name.

Impersonating agents of darkness taking my close friends or relatives' images to deceive me, and bring harm to me through my dreams, collapse with the rock of ages, in Jesus' name.

I claim all the good things, which God has revealed to me through dreams. I reject all bad and satanic dreams in the name of Jesus.

(You are going to be specific here. Place your hand on your chest and talk to God specifically about the dreams, which need to be cancelled. Cancel it with all your strength; command the fire of God to burn it to ashes.)

O Lord, perform the necessary surgical operation in my life and change all that has gone wrong in the spirit world, in Jesus' name.

I reclaim all of the good things, which I have lost as a result of defeat, in Jesus name.

I arrest every spiritual attacker and paralyze their activities in my life, in the name of Jesus.

I retrieve my stolen virtues, goodness and blessings in Jesus' name. Let all satanic manipulations through dreams be dissolved, in Jesus' name.

Let all arrows, gunshots, wounds, harassment, and opposition in my dreams return to its sender, in the name of Jesus.

I reject every evil spiritual load placed on me through dreams, in Jesus' name.

All spiritual animals (cats, dogs, snakes, and crocodiles) paraded against me, be chained and return to the sender(s) in the name of Jesus.

*ANY PROJECTION INTO AN ANIMAL SENT AGAINST ME BE TRAPPED IN THAT ANIMAL, YOU SHALL NOT RETURN BACK ALIVE, IN THE NAME OF JESUS.

Holy Ghost, purge my intestine and my blood from satanic foods and injections, in Jesus' name.

I loose myself from curses, hexes, spells, bewitchment and evil domination directed against me through dreams in the name of Jesus.

Let all satanic manipulations through dreams be dissolved in Jesus' name.

Every evil spiritual load of poverty placed on me, sender carry your own evil load in Jesus' name.

I reject every evil spiritual load of sickness placed on me through dreams in Jesus' name.

I reject every evil spiritual load of backwardness placed on me through dreams in Jesus' name.

I reject every evil spiritual load of oppression placed on me through dreams in Jesus' name.

Holy Ghost Fire, purge my intestine and my blood from satanic foods and injections.

IF YOU HAVE EATEN ANY SATANIC FOODS ASK GOD TO UPROOT IT AND VOMIT OUT.

I break every evil covenant and initiation through dreams in the name of Jesus.

Every demonic restrictions place upon my life, be removed by fire in Jesus' name

Any form of caging of my destiny be removed by fire, in Jesus Name

Chapter 6

Invisible thrones

For by Him all things were created, both in the heavens and on earth, visible and invisible, whether thrones or dominions or rulers or authorities-- all things have been created through Him and for Him. Colossians 1:16

Have you ever stepped into a house or a business and discerned the spirit of oppression resting there? In the spirit realm we don't see what's actually taking place with the natural eyes. When God open your eyes to see the activities taking place, you realize others do not see some things you see. And he put forth the form of an hand, and took me by a lock of mine head; and the spirit lifted me up between the earth and the heaven, and brought me in the visions of God to Jerusalem, to the door of the inner gate that looketh toward the north; where was the seat of the image of jealousy, which provoketh to jealousy.

And, behold, the glory of the God of Israel was there, according to the vision that I saw in the plain. Then said he unto me, Son of man, lift up thine eyes now the way toward the north. So I lifted up mine eyes the way toward the north, and behold northward at the gate of the altar this image of jealousy in the entry. He said furthermore unto me, Son of man, seest thou what they do? Even the great abominations that the house of Israel committeth here, that I should go far off from my sanctuary? But turn thee yet again, and thou shalt see greater abominations. And he brought me to the door of the court; and when I looked, behold a hole in the wall. Then said he unto me, Son of man, dig now in the wall: and when I had digged in the wall, behold a door. And he said unto me, Go in, and behold the wicked abominations that they do here. So I went in and saw; and behold every form of creeping things, and abominable beasts, and all the idols of the house of Israel, portrayed upon the wall round about. Ezekiel 8:3-9

It's imperative that you pray over any location that you will be conducting business and residing at. There can be spiritual (evil) thrones and (evil) altars, set up in the atmosphere and in homes, which can be breeding grounds for witchcraft. We must proactively pray to dismantle evil thrones and evil altars working against us. Remember! There are no wasted prayers. When you pray against witchcraft in your home you pull down barricades and blockage set up against you. What happens in the natural when you dismantle thrones & altars? You must command them to fall down, and roast to ashes. What happens when you do it in the spirit? Let's take a look at the Man of God from Bethel. When you are connected to Yahweh Sabbaoth (the Lord of Host) the powers working against you are defeated, and annihilated.

Prayer Capsules:
I will not pay obedience to any demonic household throne, in Jesus' name

You must have the power and authority, given to you by Jesus. It's not in your own strength that you fight this battle. And having disarmed the powers and authorities, he made a public spectacle of them, triumphing over them by the cross. Colossians 2:15

Section VII Prayer Capsules:

That if thou shalt confess with thy mouth the Lord Jesus, and shalt believe in thine heart that God hath raised him from the dead, thou shalt be saved. Roman 10:9 "Lord Jesus, I ask you to come into my life and forgive me of all my sins. I confess my sins before you this day. I denounce satan and all his works. I confess Jesus as the Lord of my life. Thank you for saving me. I believe with my heart and I confess with my mouth that you rose from the dead. I am saved. Write my name in the Lamb's book of life. I pray this prayer to the Father in the name of Jesus. Amen."

After praying these prayers each day bind up and backlash or retaliation, in Jesus name.

1. Please repent of every known sin and ask the LORD to wash you clean with the Blood of Jesus before you go into battle

2. Go into a session of praise and worship ... then wait quietly before the LORD and ask for the Holy Spirit to direct you.

3. Put on the whole armor of God (Eph 6:10-18) *Pray the Prayer Capsules Several times before moving on to the next one. You may be led to stay on one prayer capsule for several minutes, if so continue until you are released to continue. You may pray each day separately or pray all the prayer capsules each day.

Every person has a different battle they must fight. One person may have to break covenants with the spirit husband/wife, another must break evil covenants with Masonic groups; but first you have to go before God for direction in the route YOU must take. Do not be short changed by only praying what has been written in this book. You should now have better understanding to the battles you must make preparation for. Deliverance is an ongoing process; it is like peeling an onion one layer at a time.

Chapter 7 Weapons Of Warfare

Hail from Heaven

Then the Lord said to Moses, "Extend your hand toward the sky that there may be hail in all the land of Egypt, on people and on animals, and on everything that grows in the field in the land of Egypt." Ex 9:22

Prayer Point:

After the order of Moses, I extend my hand to the sky and release hail into the camp of my enemies and their possessions. Let the Hail bury every power fashioned against me and my family in Jesus name.

Great Heat

The people were scorched by the terrible heat, yet they blasphemed the name of God, who has ruling authority over these plagues, and they would not repent and give him glory. Rev. 16:9

Prayer Point:

Every power blaspheming the name of God receive judgment of God and be scorched by the terrible heat, dry up and die, in Jesus name.

Terror of the Lord

"I will send my terror before you, and I will destroy all the people whom you encounter; I will make all your enemies turn their backs to you. Ex 23:27

Prayer Point:

Every stubborn enemy pursuing me in my sleep, let the terror of the Lord strike you down in Jesus name.

Hornets

I will send hornets before you that will drive out the Hivite, the Canaanite, and the Hittite before you. Ex 23:28

Prayer Point:

O Lord, send the Hornets to drive out all of my enemies from their hiding places, in Jesus name.

Cup of the fury of the Lord

Wake up! Wake up! Get up, O Jerusalem! You drank from the cup the Lord passed to you, which was full of his anger! You drained dry the goblet full of intoxicating wine. Is 51:17

Prayer Point:

Let the fury of the Lord destroy all those who attempt to manipulate my destiny through dreams, in Jesus name.

Destroying Wind

The Lord says, I will cause a destructive wind to blow against Babylon and the people who inhabit Babylonia Jeremiah 51:1

Prayer point:

O God, My Father, send a destructive wind to sweep away every power seeking to put me in bondage, in Jesus Name.

Destroying Weapon

Then he shouted in my ears, "Approach, you who are to visit destruction on the city, each with his destructive weapon in his hand!" Ezekiel 9:1

Prayer point:

O Lord, send destruction upon every witchcraft coven mentioning my name in the night, in Jesus Name.

Judgment of Fire

Then a fire went out from the Lord and devoured the 250 men who offered incense. Number 16:35

Prayer Point:

O God, After the order Elijah, let fire fall upon those offering incense to idols on my behalf, in Jesus name.

God as a Consuming Fire

Understand today that the Lord your God who goes before you is a devouring fire; he will defeat and subdue them before you. You will dispossess and destroy them quickly just as he has told you Deut. 9:3

Prayer point:

O God, destroy every evil altar fashioned against me, in Jesus Name.

Arrows

Hurl lightning bolts and scatter them! Shoot your arrows and rout them! Ps 144:6

Prayer point:

O lord, send lightning bolts to every coven mentioning my name in the night, in Jesus Name.

Praise

When they began to shout and praise, the Lord suddenly attacked the Ammonites, Moabites, and men from Mount Seir who were invading Judah, and they were defeated. 2 Chronicle 20:22

Prayer point:

O God, as I offer praises to you, I thank you for destroying every power projecting against me, in Jesus name.

Thunderbolts

He rained hail down on their cattle, and hurled lightning bolts down on their livestock. Ps 78:48

Prayer point:

Let the thunderbolt of God strike down every power stealing from me in my dreams.

Vengeance of the Lord

Cry out, O nations, with his people, for he will avenge his servants' blood; he will take vengeance against his enemies, and make atonement for his land and people. Deut. 32:43

Prayer Point:

My Father God, avenge me from every evil power pursuing me in my dreams, in Jesus Name.

Fierce Wrath of God

Why should the Egyptians say, 'For evil he led them out to kill them in the mountains and to destroy them from the face of the earth? Turn from your burning anger, and relent of this evil against your people Ex 32:12

Prayer Point:

O God, let my stubborn pursuers receive the fierce wrath of God, in Jesus Name.

Fire & Brimstone

Then the LORD rained upon Sodom and upon Gomorrah brimstone and fire from the LORD out of heaven; Gen. 19:24

Prayer point:

O God, rain down fire and brimstone upon every power assigned to pollute my life, in Jesus Name.

Blindness

The Lord will also subject you to madness, blindness, and confusion of mind. You will feel your way along at noon like the blind person does in darkness and you will not succeed in anything you do; you will be constantly oppressed and continually robbed, with no one to save you. Deut. 28:28-29

Prayer point:

Every evil eye monitoring me receive irreversible blindness, in Jesus Name.

Serpent of the Lord

Even if they were to hide on the top of Mount Carmel, I would hunt them down and take them from there. Even if they tried to hide from me at the bottom of the sea, from there I would command the Sea Serpent to bite them. Amos 9:3

Prayer point:

O God, after the order of Moses let the serpent of the Lord swallow up the serpent of my enemies, In Jesus Name.

Arm of the Lord

I am ready to vindicate, I am ready to deliver, I will establish justice among the nations. The coastlands wait patiently for me; they wait in anticipation for the revelation of my power. Is 51:5

Prayer point:

O God, My Father, Vindicate me against my enemies and let them every power militating against me receive your judgment today, in Jesus Name "When you lie down, you will not be afraid; Yes, you will lie down and your sleep will be sweet." Proverbs 3:24 (NIV)

Every person has a different battle they must fight. One person may have to break covenants with the spirit husband/wife, another must break evil covenants with Masonic groups; but first you have to go before God for direction in the route YOU must take. Do not be short changed by only praying what has been written in this book. You should now have better understanding to the battles you must make preparation for. Deliverance is an ongoing process; it is like peeling an onion one layer at a time.

Deliverance shall visit your house today, in Jesus' name. Amen.

Other Books By This Author

Spiritual Warfare During Your Sleep vol. 1

Spiritual Warfare During Your Sleep Dream Diary

Dismantling Household Witchcraft

Overcoming the spirit of rejection

Barricading Your Marriage with Fire Vol. 1

The Prophet's Journal 6x9

The Prophet's Journal 8x10

How to let them Go, Co-Author Steven E. Anderson

Spiritual House Cleaning

Vindicate Me, O Lord

Visit www.wmicc.com for upcoming release dates for

Spiritual Warfare During Your Sleep vol. 3

Spiritual Warfare During Your Sleep vol. 4

Barricading Your Marriage with Fire vol. 2

Made in the USA
Coppell, TX
21 May 2021

56100996R00107